The Holbrook Years, 2002–2007

The Holbrook Years, 2002–2007

CHRISTIAN K. ZACHER

The Ohio State University Press
Columbus

Paper (ISBN: 978-0-8142-5702-9)

Type set in Minion Pro.

Contents

Karen A. Holbrook, thirteenth president of The Ohio State University.

Foreword

My qualifications for providing this account of the presidential tenure of Karen Holbrook include a long career at Ohio State and varied experience in university governance and administration. In my forty-three years here, I have served as a faculty member, center and institute director, associate dean, and department chair, and in those roles I've observed, from close and afar, seven presidencies. For several years I also directed the university's Columbian Quincentenary Committee, which let me become familiar for the first time with a presidential administration—that of Edward Jennings (1981–1990). Eight years ago I helped to create an annually offered undergraduate course, "OSU: Its History and Its World," which has taught me much about the past and present of Ohio State and about the conditions and people that help define a leader's term. And from 2005 to 2011, during the last two years of Holbrook's five-year term and the first few of the presidency of Gordon Gee, I served as Secretary of the University Senate. Much of what I know about Holbrook and my sense of her place in OSU history, then, comes both from working with her and from a knowledge of the comparative contributions of the presidents who have preceded and followed her.

My other sources for the book are the boxes of materials from Holbrook's presidency housed at the University Archives; interviews with 50 or so people—students, faculty, administrators, staff members, alumni, and members of off-campus communities—who have had varying degrees of association with her; speeches and documents authored by her; data from a host of offices across this large university; and Holbrook herself. The interpretations of what I learned from these sources are, of course, mine.

Those I have been especially dependent on and grateful to are Crystal Augsburger (who has done valuable research for the volume and prepared the index), Deborah Ballam, Julie Carpenter-Hubin, Tamar Chute, Christopher Culley, Linda Deitch, Michelle Drobik, Theresa Drummond, Katherine Eckstrand, Kevin Fitzimons, Crystal Garrett, Laura Gast, Joshua Gillespie, Rai Goerler, David Howe, Bertha Ihnat, Sue Jones, Elizabeth Lantz, Ann

Lawrence, Elizabeth Nixon, Karen Patterson, and Julie Vannatta. I have been particularly grateful to David Frantz and Ginny Trethewey for their help in understanding the larger contours of events that influenced Karen Holbrook and her administration.

Rather than tell her story chronologically I have chosen to organize the volume around the major concerns she and any university president must deal with, although within each topical chapter, subtopics and events are taken up in roughly the temporal order in which they occurred.

The appendix includes an array of information meant to illustrate different aspects of Holbrook's term. Some of the material found there has come to be expected in volumes in this series, but some of it is novel: a note exemplifying her careful, personally edited correspondence, and some pages from her weekly calendar (one from the beginning of her term, another from its end) that reveal the great variety of individuals, constituencies, and issues faced by the head of any large educational institution and by Holbrook at this institution in particular.

Holbrook appears in almost all of the photographs reproduced in the book, which seems appropriate since this narrative seeks to focus mainly on her and only secondarily on the wider worlds that surrounded her and the university. At the same time, this account should be understood not as a biography but only as an initial profile of the public work of OSU's thirteenth president. It no doubt will be refined as history absorbs the Holbrook years.

1

The New President

As the flagship educational institution in the state of Ohio, The Ohio State University provides uncommon value to the state, the nation, and the world. From 1870 forward, the university has set in place a foundation solidly based on experience and leadership in public education, and it has set in motion a vision of success marked by opportunity and great expectations as we have consistently dedicated ourselves to reaching bold and exciting goals. Our assets in this process are considerable. We move forward with a broadly embraced academic plan and diversity plan; a remarkably strong faculty, student, and staff population who are engaged in high quality work in some of the best-equipped facilities in the world; one of the largest alumni bases in the country; a strong sense of loyalty from groups internal to the university; a sense of good will from groups and individuals in the state and beyond; and an enormously successful record in private fundraising.
—*Institutional Context, from the Holbrook search committee Profile of the President of The Ohio State University*

Karen Holbrook was the first research scientist to be elected president of The Ohio State University. She was also its first woman president, following in the footsteps of the other first women at the university—students Alice and Harriette Townshend (members of the first class of the university, 1873), faculty member Alice Williams (modern languages, 1875, and a student member of the 1873 class), Trustee Alma Paterson (1924), Dean of Students Ruth Weimer Mount (1968), Provost Ann Reynolds (1979), and Dean of Home Economics Lena Bailey (1984). It took longer for a woman to be the one to preside over the university.

Holbrook, born in Des Moines, Iowa, earned undergraduate and graduate degrees in zoology at the University of Wisconsin–Madison and a PhD in biological structure from the University of Washington School of Medicine. After further training in dermatology, she began a professorial career at the University of Washington School of Medicine as an assistant professor and a subsequent administrative career, first as Vice President for Research and Dean of the Graduate School at the University of Florida and then as Senior Vice President for Academic Affairs and Provost at the University of Georgia.

The OSU Board of Trustees and its presidential search committee found in her experience many reasons to invite her to lead Ohio's flagship institution. Foremost among them was her familiarity with academic medicine, which they thought would give her a special understanding of OSU's growing medical center. She had had a career as a successful cell biologist and administrator of academic research programs, and she understood "big science." They also prized her current position as provost of a major state university, her knowledge of land-grant institutions (having been affiliated with two others—the state universities of Wisconsin and Florida as well as Georgia), her career as a faculty member and leader at two universities that were OSU's benchmarks (Washington and Wisconsin), the midwestern roots that she said she wanted to return to, and her reputation as a workaholic. As she admitted regarding the last qualification, "Those descriptions of me working 18 hours a day seven days a week are pretty accurate." The only credential that candidate Holbrook lacked was experience as president of a university of the size and complexity of OSU. Like its medical school, OSU was moving up steadily in the national rankings; whether she could help it continue to rise, as her background suggested, time and change would show.

In March of 2002, after several months of indecision, William "Brit" Kirwan, Holbrook's predecessor and the twelfth president of Ohio State, made up his mind to return to Maryland—where he had previously served as president of the University of Maryland—in order to become Chancellor of Maryland's University System. Unlike some other short-term presidents at OSU, Kirwan left lasting marks, perhaps chief among them being the Academic Plan, a map that he and most of the Board, faculty, and administrators thought necessary as a clarifying self-definition and a setting of standards and goals for the institution. Six basic, strategic actions were central to the Plan:

- build a world-class faculty;
- develop academic programs that define Ohio State as the nation's leading public land-grant university;

- improve the quality of the teaching and learning environment;
- enhance and better serve the student body;
- create a more diverse university community; and
- help build Ohio's future.

Holbrook's commitment to carry out the Plan, which was put in place in 2000, constituted another significant reason for her selection as president. But since the new president wouldn't be officially chosen until July and not actually be on the job until October 1, the Board on June 6 invited back in an interim capacity former president Edward Jennings, the professor of finance who had steered OSU through some rough fiscal waters in the past. As Board chair Jim Patterson said, Jennings was an ideal temporary leader, someone who had "great familiarity with the university and considerable experience in raising academic quality, working with faculty and addressing budget issues." Jennings also educated the Board about the search process and about the kinds of candidates he suggested Ohio State should go after. He would return in 2004, as then Board chair Tami Longaberger explained, to review "areas relating to Board effectiveness in its university oversight role."

In April, after it had become certain that Kirwan was leaving, Patterson convened and chaired an eighteen-member presidential search committee, composed of four Board members, five faculty members, two deans, two other administrators, three students, one alumnus, and one staff member. He divided the committee into small groups that were asked to define what Ohio State needed now in a president. Next, the committee agreed on a profile for Kirwan's successor that served to guide the committee and the chosen search firm, A. T. Kearney, in its work. The profile required that the new president possess six personal attributes: exemplary integrity, trustworthiness, and wisdom; superb interpersonal and communicative skills; breadth and depth of intellect; a high level of energy; tenacity and judgment; and self-confidence. In addition, the profile expected the new leader to have a demonstrated record of success in certain key areas: attracting and retaining highly talented people; building teams in ways that produce high yield results; strategically managing high achievement in an environment of change; creating, sustaining, and enhancing diversity; enabling the growth and development of internal leadership; and effectively generating resources with external constituencies. Above all, as Secretary of the Board of Trustees David Frantz recalls, the search committee was guided by an awareness that OSU's president is always an important public figure, someone who needs to feel comfortable representing the university to a variety of constituencies.

The committee was confident OSU would compete well for the best candidates, although the universities of Minnesota and Michigan and other peer institutions were also looking for new presidents at the time. A list of 100 interested applicants was eventually reduced to fifty, then to twenty, then to a dozen or so who were interviewed, and then to a final select handful. During the search, Patterson says, he was urged by Shirley Bowser, a longtime friend of Ohio State, to consider Karen Holbrook, then provost at the University of Georgia, and he and fellow Board member Dimon McFerson became impressed enough that they invited her to interview for the job. She seemed interested in being a president, and it was known that she was a finalist for that position at the University of Alabama–Birmingham and, before recently withdrawing, was one of two finalists for the presidency of Arizona State University. After her appointment, Holbrook revealed, "When I decided to begin considering opportunities away from the University of Georgia, I had one objective: to find the right fit for the final goal of my academic career—to serve as university president." She was the first candidate interviewed in Kearney's D.C. office; one participant thought that she distinguished herself from the rest of the candidates by presenting herself in a formal manner, and Patterson felt she set the bar high for all of the remaining competitors.

By early July, the candidate list was down to Holbrook and two others who finally chose to withdraw from consideration. Concerning her selection, the *Columbus Dispatch* observed that in her career to date, "Holbrook accomplished many of the same things that Ohio State's board of trustees would like to see done here." With the unanimous support of the search committee, Patterson telephoned Holbrook to make the offer (which included a salary of $325,000, higher than Kirwan's $275,000), and she accepted. Flown to Columbus on July 25, she signed a contract and was introduced to Buckeye Nation. In her acceptance speech, she outlined her goals:

> As president, I'll be particularly interested in the following areas: fostering multi-disciplinary programs, including and extending beyond science; emphasizing outreach via pre-collegiate programs to broaden the pipeline for students who see OSU as a goal—those who are the best students and those who are under-served; providing focused support for a select group of programs poised for excellence; continuing to enhance the undergraduate experience in today's context of student engagement and intentional learners with innovative programs that capitalize on the richness of the research environment; emphasizing the continuity of education over a lifetime—not education in disparate packages or separate

packages, but education that is overlapping and continuous throughout a lifetime; assuring that the faculty reward structure is aligned with institutional goals and values; and, finally, encouraging more and more of our resources to be self-earned and self-generated.

Outgoing president Kirwan said to Patterson, "You have found a good person," and, comparing her to the other candidates, Patterson called her "the best of the best."

All university presidents inherit their predecessors' achievements and problems, and Holbrook was no exception. Kirwan's Academic Plan was her most specific, largest inheritance, and it comprehensively promised progress in areas that no one would disagree were important. Some critics of the Plan found it not selective enough, and in the future Holbrook and Provost Barbara Snyder would slightly modify it, accompanying it with their Leadership Agenda, meant to refine the Plan by stressing needs that changed annually. Their Agenda highlighted three areas:

- distinctive educational experiences and opportunities for students;
- cutting-edge interdisciplinary research for short- and long-term societal benefits; and
- outreach and engagement initiatives that connect areas of academic excellence with societal needs.

Moreover, sweeping core values underpinned both the Plan and the Agenda:

- pursue knowledge for its own sake;
- produce discoveries that make the world a better place;
- ignite in our students a lifelong love of learning;
- celebrate and learn from diversity; and
- open the world to all our students.

Besides the Plan, what she inherited was a mixed agenda of both opportunities and problems. Chief and most troubling among the problems was the fact that the state of Ohio funding of the university had continued to decrease; in Kirwan's first year, it had amounted to 26.3% of the university's overall budget; as Holbrook was taking over, it stood at 21.7%. Like leaders before her at OSU and other universities, Holbrook knew that the institution had to rely more on other sources of funding. Also, there was the boisterous and sometimes uncivil "tailgate" culture that surrounded OSU football games (and those at other universities); as OSU athletic endeavors grew more and more successful and celebrated, whether or not to do something about that raucous behavior divided the campus and the broader community. In addition, what many thought of as the academic core and foundation of a university, the arts and sciences, had been organized under Kirwan and his provost, Edward Ray, into a "federation, a return almost to the single arts and sciences college that OSU knew prior to 1968"; but to many, the loose five-college structure—comprising arts, humanities, social and behavioral sciences, mathematical and physical sciences, and biological sciences—lacked real cohesion and visibility, appearing as an academic catch-all without budget authority. And perhaps most challenging for the university and its financial well-being was its booming medical center, replete with complicated organizational problems and strong personalities among its leaders, but an educational, research, and service enterprise that was essential to both the university and the community beyond it. As Board of Trustees chair Patterson put it, "Medicine is an important part of our university, and biotechnology is critical to the future of Ohio State and the state of Ohio." It was relevant for many that while at the University of Florida Holbrook had chaired an effort, co-sponsored by the government of Florida, to shape a strategy for the future of science and technology in that state. Given her academic and administrative experience, Holbrook was expected to knowledgeably clarify and guide the medical center's advancement.

Other problems abounded, but they looked fixable. There was the fairly new college-based budgeting system, enrollment-driven and dependent on specified measures of performance, though some colleges now and then got additional support via subsidies from the central administration. There was the looming cost of renovating the main library, an effort, however, that experts predicted would dramatically improve both the look and life of campus. And there was the commitment to bettering the environment in the University District, east of High Street, and in the rest of OSU's nearby neighborhoods.

Opposed to the problems were real positives bequeathed to the new president. Some she had noted in her acceptance talk, but there were others. She was supported in her determination to advance OSU across the board, in the many areas described in the Academic Plan. The university was blessed to have an undergraduate population with an ever-improving scholastic profile (which would keep on improving during her tenure) and a corresponding rise of OSU in the college popularity ratings. OSU had a varied program of outreach and engagement activities that continued to highlight its land-grant mission. All could see an ever-growing research prominence in Ohio State faculty and their programs, which Holbrook would help expand in major ways. And there existed a campus diversity plan that Holbrook would further strengthen—in concert with the advice offered her on day one by an African American colleague, English and Women's Studies professor Valerie Lee, who said, quoting renowned feminist Laurel Thatcher, "Well-behaved women never make history. So, first of all, I hope that you effectively misbehave." The University of Florida's external research funding had risen from $193 million to $256 million during her tenure there, and at the University of Georgia during her time there it had risen from $218 million to $285 million; Buckeyes hoped those changes would be repeated at OSU.

It shouldn't need saying that universities ought to pay primary attention to students, faculty, the larger community, and diversity, but the complex activities and array of demands at an institution like Ohio State require its leadership to make periodic restatements of purpose and vision that address both those and other basic concerns. That was true especially because, over a twenty-year period stretching before and after Holbrook, the university had to confront a variety of fiscal pressures, and in so doing it engaged in serious struggles to define itself more precisely and adjust its aims and direction. The Academic Plan, by itself and as modified by the Leadership Agenda, continued to guide OSU and her, but at the same time one of her strengths, as Vice Provost Randy Smith came to see while working with her, was to bring focus under the rubric of research to what otherwise might have seemed to be a disparate collection of academic emphases—the research trajectory of the university, a push for more undergraduate exposure to research, greater research collaboration among the sciences and health sciences, reform of the graduate programs that embodied the research enterprise, and, as Holbrook stressed in her July 25 arrival remarks, more cooperative research engagement with other institutions in the community. Very clearly, research was the thread among these efforts—or, in Provost Snyder's metaphor, "a steel beam that runs through and supports all we do." While the Leadership Agenda indicated the Plan-related territories she was in particular staking out, she also openly acknowledged her awareness that presidents must carry on their predecessors' work, that oftentimes one leader's initiative is not implementable until after her term ends, as when Gordon Gee's and Richard Sisson's origination of an academic plan would not see a conclusion for years, or as when budget restructuring underwent more than five years of discussion before finally being effected, by Holbrook, in 2003. President Holbrook continued as much as she initiated, and she helped change Ohio State in ways that would not be completely visible until she was gone.

2

Students

Karen Holbrook was really committed to students having direct, hands-on experiential learning opportunities. She was convinced that active learning was a valuable supplement to classroom instruction, a way of helping our students take full advantage of being at a Research I institution.
—*Martha Garland, Vice Provost and Dean for Enrollment Services and Undergraduate Education*

Physiology professor Jack Rall, who was chair of the University Senate's Faculty Council during Karen Holbrook's third year as president, and who serves now as the university's faculty ombudsman, remembers a discussion that he and other faculty had with her in the spring of 2004 about "whether undergraduates these days often work not out of necessity but rather because of a desired life style." A few months later, said Rall, "when we again met with her, she said that our conversation had stimulated her to attempt to better understand today's undergraduates. To do that, she went and read up on the question and wrote a twenty-page 'white paper' on the contemporary undergraduate. It was an example of a president who listened and realized a deficiency and attempted to correct it."

Holbrook's desire to better understand and support students was also a reflection of her dedication to the Academic Plan that had been bequeathed to her, for almost all of the goals of the Plan focused, unsurprisingly, on students in one way or another. The world-class faculty being recruited would teach the students, improved academic programs would serve them, the enhanced educational environments were being created for them, they would be enlivened by belonging to a more diverse student body, and they would benefit as citizens from the array of efforts designed to build the state of Ohio's future. Most of Holbrook's senior administrative appointments—Richard Hollingsworth (Vice President for Student Life), Robert McGrath (Vice President for Research), Patrick Osmer (Graduate Dean and Vice Provost for Graduate Studies), Gene Smith (Director of Athletics), Barbara Snyder (Executive Vice President and Provost), and Curt Steiner (Senior Vice President for Government Affairs) as well as key continuing officers like William Hall (Hollingsworth's predecessor), Martha Garland, and William Shkurti (Senior Vice President for Business and Finance) were figures tasked with what was ultimately the academic, social, athletic, and general well-being of students.

The effects of Holbrook's concern for students were matched by the constantly climbing scores of incoming undergraduates during her five years. Their ACT scores rose steadily, from 25.2 in 2002 to 27 in 2007; the percent of freshmen coming from the top 10% of their high school classes rose over those years from 32% to 53%; and the number of them designated University Scholars rose from 517 to 982. The overall freshman retention rate increased as well, from 87.7% in 2003 to 92.8% in 2008; in parallel, the African American student retention rate during those years went from 81% to 90.7% and the Hispanic student percent from 82.9% to 91%. During Holbrook's tenure, the four-year graduation rate moved up from 42.3% in 2006 to 51% in 2009. These ever-better students also received more and more prestigious awards and scholarships when they graduated: the total number of major awards (Fulbright, National Science Foundation, Marshall, and Truman, among them) rose from 24 in 2003 to 30 as Holbrook began her final year. The continually rising quality of undergraduates was fundamentally affected, of course, by the university's policy of selective admission, which had been first proposed for autumn quarters by President Jennings and then approved by the Board, effective for all quarters in Holbrook's first month on the job. Accompanying these impressive numbers was a systematic program of the assessment of student learning outcomes, aimed at demonstrating to the campus and wider audiences how conscientiously Ohio State teachers were doing their jobs.

In 2004, Holbrook and Provost Snyder created the Committee for the University-wide Review of Undergraduate Education, chaired by English professor Brian McHale, and they asked it to examine "the General Education Curriculum, the number of credit hours required for graduation, and how well OSU's undergraduate programs reflect its commitments to diversity, interdisciplinarity, research, and outreach." Few OSU committees have been given such a daunting charge, one that also sought an assessment of how the curriculum needed to be altered for a student body now markedly better than previous ones. One of its recommendations, perhaps the one most noted, was for the university to lower the required number of hours of general education courses and hours required for graduation from 190 to 181, the result of which was to help students graduate sooner and less expensively. In concert with that analysis of the curriculum, Holbrook and the previous provost, Ed Ray, had continued to endorse the idea of a federation of the Colleges of the Arts and Sciences. About the decision to restore the one college Holbrook said, "I try to listen. . . . That's part of how the Arts and Sciences Federation got put into place, because I listened. There were naysayers, but I listened to them as well, and in the end I had to make the judgment I valued."

To satisfy the increasingly better undergraduates—and maintain a curriculum and environment that would keep drawing such top-notch students to OSU—Holbrook initiated two programs, freshmen seminars (an idea she brought from the University of Georgia) and more strongly supported undergraduate research initiatives. In the view of Deborah Ballam, business professor and director of The Women's Place under Holbrook, the seminars (begun in Holbrook's second year) and the research support greatly enriched the undergraduate experience. The seminars were taught by many of the university's best instructors (and sometimes a pair of them) on a wide range of topics, and they gave beginning students close contact in small classes with engaged faculty, an experience more common to honors programs and liberal arts colleges. By Holbrook's final year in office, nearly 1,000 freshmen were enrolled in these seminars.

Her emphasis on undergraduate research, which she had stressed at the University of Georgia, arose from a wish to expose students who were new to a Research I university to the forms and processes of research long before they ordinarily would encounter them. Holbrook was always a researcher, and she was committed to introducing undergraduates to that world. In her third year as president, she reflected on what she had done for undergraduate research: "When I first came here, students thought of research as for only a few students. Now many students are embracing it. They see it's a great way to interact with faculty, a wonderful way to create knowledge, and a different kind of experiential learning that sets them up for the rest of their career." Certainly the most visible celebration of undergraduate research on campus was the Richard J. and Martha D. Denman Undergraduate Research Forum, an annual event begun before Holbrook arrived, generously funded by the Denmans. Holbrook worked to make it even more central in the lives of students than it had been; sixty students displayed their work at it when it started in 1996, and by 2007 there were 350 participants.

An increasingly internationalized student body was also a widely desired quality—at Ohio State and most other colleges—and Holbrook did much to encourage it, especially through her own travels. They included academic trips to India, China, Korea, Japan, Turkey, the United Kingdom, Brazil, Canada, Sweden, Egypt, the Netherlands, and Saudi Arabia, a great range of countries and of universities within them where she highlighted local OSU alumni and urged her hosts to continue to be hospitable to OSU students wanting to study abroad. On a 2006 trip to India, with which Ohio State had a fifty-year association and where she received an honorary degree from Punjab Agricultural University, she observed what a land-grant university president would naturally notice, that "the association of the two universities has helped Punjab to achieve a dominant place in India as a top producer of food grain. This eventually helped the country to rise from a 'hunger state' to 'food surplus' nation." The Holbrook Research Abroad Fellowship—established by her in the name of her mother, who had died soon after moving to Columbus with Holbrook—became a continuing recognition of her commitment to foreign study.

Equally important was Holbrook's establishment of the Land Grant Opportunity Scholarships program, which evoked the founding emphasis of Ohio State. By 2005 the program was making available scholarships of up to $17,000 a year to low-income, high-ability students from Ohio's eighty-eight counties.

Related initiatives during her term included the preparation of students to become global citizens as well as an encouragement for students to seek out interdisciplinary majors and minors, especially through Arts and Sciences. All these endeavors were reinforced by a new Office of Undergraduate Research, created in Holbrook's fourth year, that sought to help students find and understand the varied research opportunities that the university could offer them.

Similar in emphasis was the Honors Collegium, which was created in 2001–2002, just before Holbrook's arrival, following recommendations of the Committee to Review Honors and Scholars Programs. Because OSU was seen to "lag behind [its] peers in terms of numbers of students who receive major national fellowships and scholarships," the Collegium was established to mentor and coach "selected high-ability students to compete for prestigious post-baccalaureate fellowships, scholarships, and graduate study." The value of students' research and their practical creations was evident in all sorts of ways, perhaps most popularly in the electric car built by students in 2004, the Buckeye Bullet, the first such electric vehicle to go faster than 300 mph, on the salt flats of Utah.

Graduate studies were as much a focus of concern and investigation as the undergraduate curriculum in the Holbrook years. She and Provost

Snyder commissioned a series of reviews of doctoral programs and funding that recommended metrics for quality assessment at OSU—reviews by the Committee on Graduate Education (the so-called Freeman Committee), the Committee to Review the Graduate School (the Beck Committee), and subsequent implementation and ranking committees. These were bold evaluations, not made before, that led to hard-nosed internal ratings of all OSU doctoral programs and collective identifications of those deemed most and least deserving of continuing support. They quickly became national models of such rigorous assessment. And the President and Provost were as concerned about graduate student lives, supporting the move in 2006 of the Graduate Compensation and Benefits Committee to more visible status as a University Senate committee. In the same year, Holbrook decided that the university would henceforth cover 75% of graduate associates' health insurance costs and 50% of that for their eligible dependents.

Students have full lives to pursue, not just programs and degrees, and during Holbrook's term the university paid broad attention to helping develop those lives. The decision to replace the student union with an impressive new one on the same location was hers. Under her guidance, OSU vastly increased the capacity of its information technology support for students and improved the quality and number of campus classrooms. "Carmen," an online course management system (and the Latin word for "song" that is part of the title of the university's alma mater), usefully came into the lives of students and faculty members in Holbrook's third year. It allowed students to communicate with teachers and classmates as well as finish classwork online. Student Information Services began to grow under the watchful eye of Vice Provost Garland, and the lobby of the building that houses Student Information Services (later called Student Academic Services) would be named for Garland upon her retirement.

Perhaps the most visible alteration of the physical campus in Holbrook's time was the renovation of the fourteen-acre Oval, that protected pastoral remnant of the nineteenth-century Neil family farm out of which the land grant institution and its campus had grown. Carried out by landscape architect Michael Von Valkenburg, it was a revision of the revered middle space of Ohio State—the place where students read, play, tan, and debate itinerant preachers—a revision that aimed to make the old new while, as *OnCampus* reported, abiding by several principles: that the Oval should be maintained as a unified greenspace, its visual impact enlarged by a simplifying of the landscape, its furnishings kept simple and timeless, and the parking around it made unobtrusive.

Holbrook's presidency also witnessed the near completion of the renovated Thompson Library, a project that, once finished, would reestablish the library as the Oval's western anchor and the campus' academic center. The project began before Holbrook, with a $5 million gift from Thomas E. and Patricia A. Duke Robinson and a $2 million gift from the Paul G. Duke Foundation, but Holbrook played a pivotal role in assuring that the renovation moved forward, and under her leadership the rest of the needed funding was found—$7 million in university funds, $71 million in state funds, $23 million in further private gifts, and a notable $9 million contribution from the OSU Department of Athletics. Football coach Jim Tressel and his wife also contributed their time, presence, and more funding to the renovation.

Adjacent to the Columbus campus on its north, east, and south sides is the University District, where the largest number of OSU students live. From the 1870s on, when OSU presidents resided near 15th and High Street, across from the student-densest part of the University District, they have kept a close eye on the UD, because the lively student partying there can lead to behavior that breaks the law, undermines safety, and gives the university an unwanted reputation. The OSU–University of Michigan football game, perhaps the greatest college rivalry in the country, over the years has regularly included such partying, but the resultant behavior around the November 23, 2002, OSU-Michigan game in Columbus—scarcely two months into Holbrook's term—became riotous in nature, and it prompted a presidential response that led the larger Buckeye community to take sides either for or against her decisions. Any account of Holbrook's firm response to that event belongs appropriately in this recollection of her relationship with students, because college athletics are historically part of student life, however socially exaggerated they have become in the American scene. Rioters—most of them, it turned out, not OSU students—were arrested for overturning cars, setting fires, and creating widespread mayhem, and on the recommendation of the Office of Student Affairs and campus police, Holbrook ordered open container and underage drinking laws to be strictly enforced thereafter. As she said in a letter to a Buckeye fan who had experienced similar offensive behavior at the OSU-Wisconsin game that year in Madison, "there is a popular culture operating on the premise that laws and rules are suspended when football is the day's entertainment." And as she said to OSU fans, "You can't have a double standard. You can't tell the students we're going to come down hard on underage drinking and then look the other way at the open container law. And that's what made people very unhappy, because what it did was cut down on the big bars and the tailgating." She accompanied her decisions with a nationally noted conference on student game behavior and riot culture and with appointment of a task force to look at long-term solutions. Her actions were widely applauded; she was honored by the Center for College Health and Safety with a President's Leadership Group award for what she did to create a healthier game-day atmosphere.

Some students, alumni, and tailgaters and even a few Trustees opposed her decision (and some people booed her in public and heckled her through the media); but she was backed by most of the Trustees, and especially two of its Board chairs, Jim Patterson and Tami Longaberger, as well as OSU administrators, staff, and faculty, a majority of Columbus residents, and the officers responsible for campus peace and safety. It was definitely her hardest public decision, one that, fairly or not, would be the thing many would remember about her presidency. Looking back at the event and her decision five years later, she said, "It's a tough thing to take a tough stand, and my guess is if a man had done it, they'd say 'That took courage' instead of 'That was stupid'." Other OSU presidents, including Gordon Gee and Edward Jennings, called her decision "brave" and thanked her for having made it. They were echoed by Vice President Bill Hall, who said, "Taking on the issue of game-day behavior was a very, very bold decision on her part." Some critics said she should have consulted more widely before making her decision; others thought it was one she properly made on her own. As Vice President Robert McGrath put it, her action brought her both criticism and respect.

During 2002–3, severe crimes plagued the areas near campus, marring Holbrook's inaugural year. Three people (one a student) were shot execution style in a house in the District. Fire destroyed another house, killing five people (two of them OSU students), set by an arsonist who is yet to be found. Crimes like these certainly can occur anywhere, not only on college campuses, but they often become the sensational stories that the media favor. However, halfway through her term, the *Columbus Dispatch* opined that she had "handled each difficulty with grace and quiet strength."

Allegations of misguided booster involvement with student athletes led to better mentoring of boosters, and less than careful operation of SASSO (the Student-Athlete Support Services Office) led Holbrook to have SASSO and its advising arm report to undergraduate dean Garland in order to offer those students more expert advising.

In 2003, it also fell to Holbrook to help Ohio State weather the accusations and unruly behavior of football star Maurice Clarett. An Ohio high school standout, Clarett played only one year for Ohio State, contributing mightily to its 14–0 season and the 2002 BCS National Championship, which OSU earned in the Fiesta Bowl largely because Clarett made a crucial defensive play and in overtime scored the winning touchdown. Off the field, however, Clarett alleged misbehavior on the part of OSU administrators, and a teaching assistant accused him of receiving unfair advantage from a professor (a claim that an OSU investigation showed was without foundation). Clarett's filing of a false police report about goods he said were stolen from his car launched an NCAA investigation that resulted in Clarett being suspended for the 2003 football season. Clarett even sued the NFL to gain early entry in the draft after he left Ohio State. (There followed an unsuccessful stint with the NFL Denver Broncos, mixed success at semi-professional football, an arrest in 2006 for armed robbery, jail, early release in 2010, and re-enrollment for a time at Ohio State.)

Holbrook also presided over the controversial firing of basketball head coach Jim O'Brien for providing money to a recruit and the NCAA investigation it triggered. That investigation revealed that student-athletes received impermissible benefits in our football and men's and women's basketball programs and also revealed that men's basketball players received improper academic assistance.

The OSU/NCAA investigation that began with coach Jim O'Brien, however, led to the creation of better booster education, institution of a dual reporting line of the compliance office to both the Department of Athletics and the Office of Legal Affairs, and the removal of SASSO from the Athletic Department to Office of Academic Affairs.

She also presided over the retirement of longtime Athletic Director Andy Geiger. Geiger was generally acknowledged to be one of the best athletic directors in the country. His management sustained thirty-six sports; he hired the three chief coaches, two of whom are still in their jobs today—Jim Foster (women's basketball), Jim Tressel (football), and Thad Matta (men's basketball); he managed the Clarett and O'Brien cases; he directed a spectacular expansion of campus athletic facilities—the Steelwood Athletic Training Facility, the Bill Davis Baseball Stadium, the Schottenstein Center, the Jesse Owens Memorial Stadium, and the McCorkle Aquatic Pavilion; and he was engaged with the Columbus community in ways that extended far beyond athletics. "I couldn't be more proud of Andy Geiger," she told NCAA president Myles Brand, and she praised Geiger for his leadership in getting everyone to pull together "to take us through some difficult situations." Replacing Geiger would be a real task for Holbrook. Reflecting back on these events a year later, she told a reporter, "Coming on, when you haven't dealt with these kinds of things before, in the volume that I did, it was hard." But before long, the president and OSU sports fans would have a new AD, a new basketball coach, and more football prowess to cheer about—as well as a university whose student profile and faculty research accomplishments kept it constantly on the rise.

3

The Faculty

The work you do radiates out from this campus and touches this state, touches people who will never sit in your classroom and never knock on your office door. Hope radiates from this place because of the work you do each day.
—*E. Gordon Gee, eleventh president of the university, speech to the faculty*

It is difficult to talk about a university's faculty separate from the faculty members' research (the subject of the next chapter) or from the students that the faculty teach (the subject of the previous chapter). Faculty are the continuity of the institution, the reason the students are here, the people whose scholarly productivity and teaching give the school its standing. The faculty do much of the university's academic business, through its governance system and other committees and task forces, and they make the critical judgments about students' and colleagues' performances. The traditional divide between faculty and administrators hides the fact that administrators usually were faculty before they were administrators, often see themselves as still part of the faculty, and sometimes return to it.

In Karen Holbrook's time at Ohio State, she witnessed faculty involved in the crucial business of the university. To quote from one of her lists, she found faculty engaged with "all-university activities such as Senate, search committees, general topic committees assembled to develop a strategic plan or consider revision of the undergraduate curriculum, and institutional accreditation activities." It was no surprise that the Commission on Research, operating five years before her arrival, repeated injunctions heard through the years back to the university's founding, when it recommended that "investment in faculty be the number one strategy of the University," a decision that also meant "recruiting well, retaining faculty selectively, setting expectations in line with university goals, and providing faculty with competitive administrative and financial support to perform optimally." One way to insure improvement in the quality of faculty is to give them good raises, and between 2003 and 2008, annual faculty raises increased over every previous year except once. Holbrook also did what she could to advance the compensation of faculty in relation to OSU's benchmark institutions.

Of course, departments and deans, rather than presidents, hire faculty, but Holbrook was a president who strongly supported those objectives. "[A]t her core," thought 2004–5 Board of Trustees Chair Tami Longaberger, Holbrook was a teacher and a researcher. Indeed, the first of the six strategies of the 2000 Academic Plan, which she shepherded from her inauguration on, was "to build a world-class faculty," and her accompanying Leadership Agenda echoed that aim. Throughout her term, faculty were recognized as essential to the improving character of the university, for both their brains and their participation in what binds the administration and the faculty and the students together for the progress of the institution—shared governance.

What seemed to animate Holbrook the most about academic life was the faculty's research. Having been vice president for research at the University of Florida, a position she would return to at the University of South Florida upon leaving OSU, it was natural that the faculty who prominently did research were of chief concern to her. While some faculty members may have felt she was not generally too approachable or gregarious, others found her voluble when she was discussing research. Professor Jack Rall thought she spoke about others' research and her own with more enthusiasm than she showed for a lot of other topics.

Various statistics testify to the results of her successful dedication to improving the faculty and their research profile at the university. From 2002 to 2007, the number of Ohio State faculty inducted into the American Academy for the Advancement of Science increased remarkably, from two new members in 2000 to seventy-two between 2002 and 2007, an average of twelve a year. OSU membership in the prestigious National Academy of Science likewise boomed: from 1975 to 2001, the year before she assumed office, OSU contributed four new members, but between five and nine new OSU members were admitted in each of Holbrook's five years. It was widely believed that Holbrook used her service on the boards and committees of learned scientific organizations such as these to highlight faculty from Ohio State and promote their membership.

Certainly her personal and presidential stress on research across the campus encouraged the hiring of faculty who were acclaimed researchers, an outcome acknowledged in the increased numbers of faculty who were honored during her tenure with the title Distinguished University Professor. As well, from 1984, the year of the inception of the Ohio Eminent Scholar (OES) program, until 2001, OSU received thirteen OES appointments, but Holbrook oversaw the appointment of nearly that many—eleven—in her five years alone. So, too, the President's and Provost's Advisory Committee (PPAC)—founded in the late 1980s and composed of the Distinguished University Professors and Ohio Eminent Scholars—expanded during her term; she and Provost Snyder continued the practice of meeting periodically with that group to obtain research-related advice (for instance, asking the PPAC to assess the progress of the programs to which she and her provost awarded Targeted Investment in Excellence status).

Other statistics about faculty in the Holbrook years are equally telling. From 2003 through 2008, OSU hired a total 269 tenured or tenure-track faculty, in each of those five years adding more than in the previous year. That was the result of a major effort to undertake specific kinds of hiring in order to accomplish the first goal of the Academic Plan: "Over the next three to five years, recruit at least 12 faculty members who have attained or have the potential to attain the highest honors in their disciplines, concentrating these appointments in areas of strategic focus." By 2005, Holbrook could say, "We DO have a world-class faculty. The achievements of both our junior and senior faculty are extraordinary, and include a wide array of awards, prizes, medals, honorary degrees, alumni awards, grants, and fellowships that recognize their expertise in their disciplines, their success in teaching innovation, scholarship and research, and service."

One reason OSU's faculty profile remained high was that, as she noted in her 2005 State of the University Address, she had earmarked special funding ($1.5 million in 2004–5 alone) to make counteroffers in order to hold onto the superb faculty OSU had worked so hard to hire. In collaboration with the deans of Humanities and Arts, for instance, she also set aside a generous multiyear competitive seed and innovation grants fund for faculty in those areas—disciplines that have relatively meager sources of external funding—and this special support stimulated those faculties in a variety of research enterprises.

Another important sign of her dedication to faculty was her support for creation of the position of research faculty member, a new category at OSU, which the University Senate approved in 2004. While some critics felt that doing research should continue to be expected of every regular faculty member at the university, the proposal for research faculty argued that these faculty, who did mainly research, were essential to a research university and that its establishment was an urgent priority in both Holbrook's Leadership Agenda and the Academic Plan. As Stephen Pinsky, physics professor and chair of the Senate Steering Committee during Holbrook's time, observed, OSU needed such a track to lure high-powered research faculty to campus to run the ever increasing big science programs.

Holbrook's attention to faculty knowingly included a concern for their work life. In collaboration with Board chair Tami Longaberger, she labored to make available to faculty, staff, and students (including same-sex domestic partners) new sponsored dependent insurance coverage. In proposing the plan to the Board, which endorsed it unanimously, Holbrook reported, "Our campus community cares deeply about this issue. . . . In addition to enhancing our ability to compete for the best faculty, staff, and students, this benefits program also serves our commitment to diversity and allows us to provide a supportive environment for everyone on the Ohio State campus." Her approval of a new parental leave policy, giving parents paid time off after the birth or adoption of a child, was a decision made in the same spirit. These improvements were part of Holbrook's broad interest in bettering work life for the entire community.

Perhaps the most novel feature of this concern was her support for Your Plan for Health, a Human Resources initiative, which she described in her 2005 Academic Plan update as a comprehensive plan that will "promote personal health awareness and health management. To be implemented from 2006 to 2010, the new plan will provide support and technological resources to help individuals improve their health and wellness, while ultimately helping Ohio State manage costs."

All of this attention to the working conditions of everyone in the OSU family was also highlighted in the many recommendations arising out of the Faculty Career Enhancement Committee, which she appointed in 2004 and whose report made valuable recommendations "for integrating professional and personal life. Intended to support the professional development of women and minority faculty members, and associate professors especially, these recommendations provide guidance on mentoring, peer evaluation, professional leave, recruitment, and support for interdisciplinary activities." The many recommendations coming out of the Enhancement Committee also reflected Holbrook's determination to make the quotidian conditions of work and life of everyone at OSU more flexible and enlightened. Holbrook endorsed a number of them, and others found favor with successive university leaders.

Faculty not only drove the teaching and research of the institution; as partners in shared governance they also contributed significantly to the development of the institution's policies, mainly through the legislative work of the University Senate and its Faculty Council, the faculty caucus of the Senate. Acting as a bridge from the Senate to the President and other central administrators was the four-member faculty leadership, composed of the chair and chair-elect of Faculty Council, the chair of the Senate Steering Committee, and the Secretary of the Senate. Faculty also composed the core of the major curriculum reviews of her time—the Freeman and McHale committees. At Holbrook's request, Faculty Council reviewed the need for the defunct position of Secretary of the Faculty and recommended its abolition, and it was in 2005 that she encouraged the first discussions about inviting faculty to serve on a committee of the Board of Trustees, which would come about in 2010 with the Board's appointment of comparative studies professor David Horn to the Board's committee on Academic Affairs and Student Life. With her agreement, Faculty Council initiated a committee that performed annual evaluations of central administrators (vice presidents and vice provosts) and their offices. The Secretary of the Board of Trustees, David Frantz, while appointed by the Board, was a faculty member who worked closely with Holbrook as she strove to enhance relationships on and off campus.

The new Buckeye Village Child Care Center, designed by OSU faculty member Kay Bea Jones and architecture alumni Andrew Rosenthal and George Acock—who was beginning to rival earlier architect Howard Dwight Smith in the number of campus buildings credited to him—symbolized those intentions. As Holbrook said at its opening, the center would provide single parents living on a low income "with a supportive environment that offers childcare, mentoring, financial planning, employment assistance, and other services. It is a sound investment in their future and in our community."

Holbrook also did what she could to advance the compensation of faculty in comparison with that of faculty at OSU's benchmark institutions. She encouraged faculty—especially women and minorities—to develop themselves as leaders, most notably through the President's and Provost's Leadership Institute, born out of The Women's Place in 2005. Many of these faculty-co-sponsored initiatives resulted from Holbrook's ability to work cooperatively with two different Senate Secretaries and ten different elected faculty leaders. What helped keep her and the faculty's policy issues front and center were the regular monthly meetings of free-flowing discussion that she, like presidents before and after her, regularly hosted in her office with those faculty leaders.

Two enormous campus undertakings dear to the faculty that were begun, though not completed, in her time were the renovation of Thompson Library and the re-establishment of a College of Arts and Sciences. Brit Kirwan launched the library project, but, as Senior Vice President for Business and Finance Bill Shkurti stressed, Holbrook "played a critical role in getting the project funded, designed, and constructed." The new library and its symbolic location in the middle of the campus reminded all of the centrality of books and knowledge in the life of a university; similarly, the act of re-gathering the arts and sciences acknowledged the foundational importance of those pursuits to the university. Faculty associated the start-up of these initiatives with the Holbrook presidency, and the development of both would prompt renewed considerations of the essential importance of research to a public, land-grant university. An attention to research was, finally, the hallmark of Holbrook's leadership, and it deserves to be examined in detail.

Karen Holbrook introduced in 2002 as the new president, with husband James Holbrook. Source: The *Columbus Dispatch* Photo Archives.

At the 2002 Nationwide and Ohio Farm Bureau 4-H Center ground-breaking, with (from left) interim OSU president Edward H. Jennings, Chair of the Board of Trustees James Patterson, and 4-H member Ryan Hamilton. Source: The *Columbus Dispatch* Photo Archives.

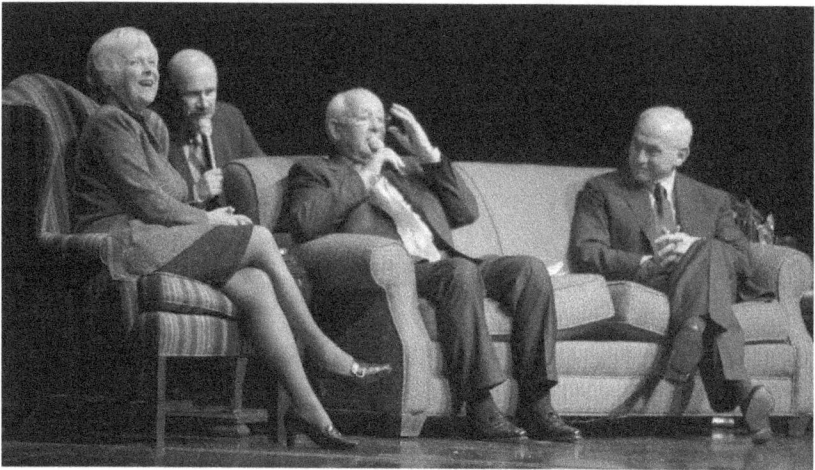

Hosting former Soviet Union President Mikhail Gorbachev, with Leslie Wexner and In-terpreter Pavel Palazchenko, in 2002. Source: The *Columbus Dispatch* Photo Archives.

Speaking at Governor Robert Taft's 2003 Third Frontier campaign press conference.
Source: The *Columbus Dispatch* Photo Archives.

Football player Maurice Clarett scoring a touchdown in the 2003 Fiesta Bowl. Source: OSU Photo Services.

Accepting the 2002 National Championship trophy from head football coach Jim Tressel at a 2003 Buckeye basketball game. Source: The *Columbus Dispatch* Photo Archives.

Speaking with new head basketball coach Thad Matta at the 2004 news conference welcoming him to OSU. Source: The *Columbus Dispatch* Photo Archives.

Speaking to the media with OSU Athletics Director Gene Smith about a notice of allegations from the NCAA in 2005. Source: The *Columbus Dispatch* Photo Archives.

With Vice President for Business and Finance William Shkurti, following a 2004 Board of Trustees meeting. Source: The *Columbus Dispatch* Photo Archives.

With benefactor Leslie Wexner and Wexner Center Director Sherri Geldin, recognizing the 2004 Wexner Prize recipient Issey Miyake. Source: OSU Photo Services.

Conducting a fireside chat with students in 2004 at the Kuhn Honors House. Source: OSU Photo Services.

With the 2004 Board of Trustees. Source: OSU Photo Services.

Sharing a laugh with Secretary of the Board of Trustees David Frantz following her 2005 State of the University speech. Source: The *Columbus Dispatch* Photo Archives.

4

Research

At its best, research is part of the continuing quest for deeper understanding of the universe in all its infinite beauty, infinite complexity. Research is short-hand for critical inquiry, for constant and relentless and enduring quest. . . . The philosopher whose tools are the library, paper and pencil is as much a part of the action as the astronomer and the physicist, each served by tools of great complexity and great cost.
—*Harold L. Enarson, tenth president of the university*

Karen Holbrook's supporters and critics both agree that her most striking success as president lay in her championing of research across the university, which resulted in a significantly higher national research profile for Ohio State. Describing her efforts in this arena necessitates repeating some of the story told in the previous chapter about faculty as well as reminding ourselves that the university's varied outreach and delivery of benefits to the rest of society are often inseparable from research and certainly depend on it. Thus, any account of a Research I land-grant university's means and goals ought naturally to begin with its research achievements, and that is especially true for any account of Karen Holbrook's efforts at OSU. Echoing the view of Board of Trustees chair Tami Longaberger that Holbrook was above all a teacher and a researcher, former president Edward Jennings said that "[r]esearch was her strong suit and she deserves major credit for its expansion at Ohio State, not only in quantity but in quality as well." As geography professor and vice provost W. Randy Smith has noted, "Faculty at a research university respond very positively to leadership that shows how research is linked to all that we do. Karen Holbrook did so."

In choosing her, the Board was aware of Holbrook's accomplishments as vice president for research at the University of Florida and as provost at the University of Georgia, at both of which institutions she dramatically raised the levels of external research funding received by faculty and their programs. She clearly believed she knew enough to do the same for Ohio State; in fact, in 2004, she revealed that prior to coming to OSU she was aware of the school's greater research potential. During the previous several years, as she told an interviewer, "I reviewed Ohio graduate programs in the biomedical and life sciences and was a reviewer for Hayes Investment Fund grants for the Ohio Board of Regents. I had a great opportunity to see the research capabilities of Ohio State and the other public institutions in Ohio." In an essay she titled "Fixing the Fragmented University: Decentralization with Direction," a vision for Ohio State that is also important for understanding Holbrook's awareness of her place in OSU history, she underscored the value of the 1997 Ohio State Commission on Research Report for developing a renewed research emphasis at OSU. In the essay, she strongly supports the Commission's recommendation that "the University would need to improve the existing economics of sponsored research (e.g., F&A ratio, larger grants), restructure some of the existing investments in research and reallocate in focal areas, enhance the University's investment in development activities, establish research alliances, and secure additional dollars from the state." Gains in research funding were essential to OSU's determination to become, in the words of Provost Snyder, the premier public land-grant research university in the nation.

During her presidency, Holbrook implemented most of these recommendations and made interdisciplinary research, in particular, one of her main areas of academic emphasis. In "Fixing the Fragmented University" she praises the earlier Gee/Sisson administration's Academic Enrichment Program for incentivizing interdisciplinary centers and programs that could boost the university's reputation. Her vice president for research, Bob McGrath, has stressed that she gave great support to interdisciplinary projects because she was aware that the main federal funders of such interdisciplinary projects in the sciences, the National Institutes of Health and the National Science Foundation, pointedly favored such efforts. And, as she observed in her 2005 update of the Academic Plan, "Our distinction as a research university rests in no small measure on our ability to help our faculty and students make connections between fields of study and bring to bear the insights from many disciplines in seeking solutions to hunger, disease, illiteracy, resource usage, threats to the environment, and other issues facing the global community. To meet these challenges," she said, "the Office of Research has established the

Large Interdisciplinary Seed Grant Program to spur the development of extra-mural grant proposals for major interdisciplinary initiatives."

At this time, she was about halfway through her term, near its peak, and with good reason she could brag about the large and complex research initiatives that her administration had undertaken. Her list was a full one. The renovation of the Thompson Library (once called the Main Library), the research laboratory for humanists and social scientists, was being readied for a fall 2006 reconstruction. "New curricular offerings and degree programs at Ohio State are identifying us as a leader in interdisciplinary research," she reported, "as well as in teaching and learning." "Partnerships with the Battelle Memorial Institute," she said, "are allowing us to collaborate in tackling such issues as health and the environment and privacy and development." More successfully than any earlier president, Holbrook had reached south across King Avenue to the nationally prominent research facility and worked to link Ohio State and Battelle in a variety of collaborations, among them the eventual STEM-focused Metro Early College High School, jointly designed by OSU, Battelle, and the Columbus Educational Council. Cooperative research endeavors with Battelle and other nearby research institutions were creating a site of activity that five years later Battelle CEO Jeffrey Wadsworth would compare favorably with Silicon Valley, North Carolina's Research Triangle, and Boston's Route 128. In part, these collaborations succeeded because of the strong personal ties Holbrook developed with then Battelle president Carl Kohrt.

First-rate research space had expanded on campus, with plans in place for a Biomedical Research Tower, a Physics Research Building, Scott Laboratory, and a Psychology Building, all of which were finished in 2005 or 2006. Following a broad competition across the university, the Targeted Investment in Excellence (TIE) funding program had been launched, by Holbrook and Snyder, intended to "support high profile programs that would bring distinction to the colleges and to the university and move the program(s) upward in the rankings." Forty-one proposals were submitted in the TIE competition; the President and Provost decided to fund ten of them, all projects that were global in significance and pressingly practical in their promised outcomes. What was novel about the competition was the requirement that every one of the thirty-one proposals not funded centrally be funded by the proposers' home colleges. They all also had to promise to have an economic impact on the state of Ohio, a stipulation also central to Governor Taft's Third Frontier awards competition, which from 2003 to 2008 yielded more than $136 million to OSU or jointly to OSU and its collaborators. The ten TIE projects were:

1. Climate, Water, and Carbon Program
2. Mathematical Biosciences Institute
3. Public Health Preparedness Program
4. Center for Cosmology and Astro-Particle Physics
5. Center for Energy, Sustainability and the Environment
6. Advanced Materials Initiative
7. Population and Health Initiative
8. Translational Plant Sciences Initiative
9. Music, Media and Enterprise
10. Micro-RNA Project

Holbrook was dedicated to supporting research in all disciplines, not only in the sciences, as she showed in her allocation of special funding to researchers in the humanities and arts. She was also the force behind the university and College of Arts agreement to display the work of artists in downtown Columbus and provide public programming in the new Urban Arts Space at the revitalized Lazarus department store site. Eager to stress research and to work cooperatively with partners throughout the community, OSU became conspicuous in its association with the Program for International Homeland Security, the Third Frontier initiative of Governor Taft, technology transfer through SciTech, the research components of the near-to-campus Weinland Park project, and other efforts co-sponsored with Battelle.

Although she chose not to give it the autonomous budget authority many thought it needed—and that it would receive from the next administration—she and Provost Snyder supported the plan for a single, unified College of Arts and Sciences, a plan that pointed toward that future day when its 1,000-member faculty would contribute mightily to the university's research profile. So, too, on her watch the merger of Education and Human Ecology presented OSU with a combined college that could pursue ever more interdisciplinary activity. Reflective of this support for research across the university was the Holbrook administration's proposal, approved by the University Senate in 2004, for creation of a non-tenured regular research faculty track. It was intended to "facilitate the hiring of senior, established scholars who are interested primarily in research and for whom tenure is no longer important."

Holbrook's expansion of support for research was measurable in particularly visible ways: technology licensing revenue increased from $828,000 to $947,000 between 2002 to 2006; and between her first and last years as president, total research expenditures at OSU rose from $432 million to $720 million, prompting the National Science Foundation to rank OSU among the top

10 public universities in research expenditures and sixth in the country among all universities for industry-sponsored research.

Most of these new higher rankings would not have been possible without developments in the medical part of campus. Medical schools, like athletic programs, can be sources of pride as well as nervous challenges for university presidents, and in her five years Holbrook encountered experiences at once satisfying and difficult in both those arenas. Medicine and the world of research related to it especially occupied her attention. While she was hired because of her long familiarity with medical centers and hospitals, she had not encountered a medical environment as large as Ohio State's. Its challenges took several forms. She inherited various problems in the fast-growing Medical Center at a time when such centers and their hospitals were heavily competing regionally and nationally for patients and rankings. Some observers, in fact, considered the Center dysfunctional. Like many a medical dean, Dr. Fred Sanfilippo—also senior vice president, executive dean for health sciences, and CEO of the Medical Center, who was hired from John Hopkins before Holbrook's arrival—had a community presence that rivaled hers. She, for example, held a seat on the board of Columbus Partnership, the most powerful group of local leaders—and so did Sanfilippo. He was seen both positively and negatively as an ambitious figure, and his entrepreneurial spirit found an echo in the desires of some (though not all) members of the Board of Trustees.

The combined budget of the Center and the several OSU hospitals was nearing the point of being half of the university's budget (both half of its costs as well as half of its revenue), and so the medical campus at the southwest corner of OSU constituted a crucial part of the university's fiscal world. While Holbrook knew what the physicians and medical scientists were teaching and researching at the Medical Center, she found its budget not always transparent and its management and structure not always responsive. The financial plan that underpinned Sanfilippo's blueprint for the future seemed to some not as solid as it might have been, although the Board of Trustees ultimately did approve it. Finally, like many a dean and medical CEO, Sanfilippo sought centralized control of the medical campus (including the new cancer center).

One form of that centralizing, in the words of OSU historian Bob Tenenbaum, was "the creation of UMC Partners, a non-profit corporation designed to identify business opportunities and find commercial funding for science and research emerging from the OSU Medical Center." The Board of Trustees' charge to the UMC Partners was to create an infrastructure that could support partnerships for profit and not-for-profit. Unfortunately, as Board Secretary

David Frantz has said, "Partners never fulfilled its promise." It did not identify and implement any business partnerships that would allow it to raise needed revenue, and as Board member Jo Ann Davidson has noted, "The Partners didn't want to be impeded by the limitations of the University's debt capacity." Partners was dissolved in fall 2007.

Just how a medical center fits with the rest of a university—not an easy issue in the best of times—inevitably became a larger and larger issue at various administrative and board levels on campus, and it probably would have taken a president with the political skills of a Lyndon Johnson to resolve all the elements that figured in the objectives and contentions of the various parties in the Medical Center. Serious discord between the James Cancer Center programs and both the rest of the Medical Center and the campus generally spilled beyond the confines of OSU into the larger community. Even the university's building plan was delayed when the Medical Center argued that it deserved more space. Eventually, those tensions led the Board of Trustees to instruct the university general counsel, Christopher Culley, to try to bring alignment between the James and the Medical Center.

Sanfilippo departed OSU the same year that Holbrook did, leaving behind a record of several prominent hires and the identification of six signature programs that were designed to contribute to the university's reputation—Cancer, Critical Care, Heart, Imaging, Neurosciences, and Transplant. In a later article that offered his retrospective assessment of what he had achieved at OSU, Sanfilippo made the case for his direction having improved OSU's academic health center across the board during his tenure, in leadership culture, employee and customer satisfaction, and academic, clinical, and financial performance. Some would agree and others would not.

How well Holbrook presided over the fortunes of the Medical Center, like how well she handled the imposition of tailgating restrictions at football games, became a measure of her leadership for fans and critics. Bill Shkurti believes the Medical Center "managed to survive financially despite her difficulty in controlling the dean," but also that "her financial prudence helped put the university in a better position to weather the financial collapse of 2008–09." Since Holbrook's departure, the Center has become steadily more prosperous. Without a doubt, its ever-growing funded research has contributed to the entire university's higher research profile. Research was Holbrook's passion, and Ohio State's ranking as a public research university has benefitted importantly from her understanding and leadership of the institution's overall research enterprise.

5

A More Diverse Campus

I believe that we need to protect the rich social diversity of our species and act on the assumption that every culture and every individual has, or may have, important gifts that can benefit us all. We educators have the professional duty to seek out their gifts and talents wherever they can be found and to nurture them.
—*Mac Stewart, Vice Provost and Chief Diversity Officer*

If, according to the OSU Senate Diversity Committee, diversity refers to the inclusive representation of multiple (ideally all) groups within it, then increasing the diversity of students, staff, faculty, and administrators has been a longtime central goal of the university. Holbrook's immediate predecessor also was a forceful advocate of diversity, and it was fitting that Ohio State's new institute be called the Kirwan Institute for the Study of Race and Ethnicity. Through a number of other significant efforts with long-term impact, Holbrook furthered the university's progress toward that goal.

The Academic Plan that she embraced had as its fifth strategy a commitment to create a diverse university community, and she supported it with two important initiatives: first, a determination to hire "at least five to ten women and five to ten minority faculty at a senior level each year for five years," and, second, to "recruit, support, and retain to graduation larger numbers of academically able minority students." In her 2005 update of the 2000 Plan, Holbrook could report that, following a variety of recruitment efforts out of the Office of Minority Affairs aimed at the African American and Hispanic communities, in that year OSU had exceeded its objective, having hired seventeen women and twelve minority regular faculty members. The second initiative also was fulfilled: 81%

of African American and 82% of Hispanic first-year students had returned for a second year in 2003. By 2005 those figures had improved to, respectively, 88% and 87%, and by 2007 they would improve even more, to 90% and 91%.

In the same update, she could also point to the 2005 establishment of the President and Provost's Leadership Institute (PPLI), "a collaboration of the Women's Place and the Office of Human Resources that was meant to develop a pool of potential leaders from groups that have been traditionally under-represented in key administrative positions." Professor Deborah Ballam, later vice provost and director of The Women's Place, was the prime mover behind PPLI, supported strongly by Holbrook and Snyder. Since its founding, the Institute has graduated 100 members (84 of them women).

Ballam's view of Holbrook is that "she gave great hope and inspiration to many at Ohio State that women could succeed at the highest ranks. She appointed one of the most diverse senior leadership teams, both in terms of race and sex, that we ever had. She clearly was a pathbreaker for women in senior leadership. The next woman president, I am quite sure, will be introduced simply as the president and not as the 'second woman president'." Indeed, Holbrook's concern for women and their advancement in the academy was most visibly illustrated in the number of women she appointed to key leadership positions at the university—Ballam, Evie Freeman (executive dean of the regional campuses), Joan Herbers (dean of biological sciences), Deborah Merritt (director of what would become the John Glenn School of Public Affairs), and Jacqueline Royster (executive dean of the Colleges of the Arts and Sciences).

Most commentators on her presidency single out the appointment of Barbara Snyder to be provost as her most significant administrative appointment. Prior to serving as provost Snyder had been an associate dean of the Moritz College of Law, interim vice president for university relations, and vice provost for academic policy and human resources. Shortly before Holbrook resigned her position, Snyder was recruited to be president of Case Western Reserve University. Before they both left OSU, it was a distinctive fact about the university that, at the same time, its top three leaders were women—the provost, the president, and the Board of Trustees chair.

Under Holbrook's leadership, a number of other diversity-related initiatives were undertaken. One she especially highlighted was creation of the Todd Anthony Bell National Resource Center on the African American Male, which has sought to recruit and retain African American male students. Bell was an All-American football player at OSU who played in the NFL for the Chicago Bears and the Philadelphia Eagles and then finished his undergraduate degree at OSU. He had served as community affairs coordinator for the

Office of Minority Affairs and director of its resource center until his untimely death in 2005. Naming the resource center for him, said Holbrook, was appropriate since "the University is indebted to Todd for his commitment to the academic and personal success of students and his concern for our community."

In her October 2004 State of the University address to the Senate, she proudly reported on a number of other diversity initiatives. She announced there that the Trustees had agreed with her administration's decision to include sponsored dependents in the university benefits package—a decision in part influenced by recommendations of the Faculty Career Enhancement Committee. Throughout her term, Holbrook encouraged the reliance on flextime practices all across campus and on family-friendly policies, emphases apparent in the Faculty Work Environment report (2003) and that of the President's Council on Women's Issues (2004).

Judge Robert Duncan, an African American and someone familiar with OSU attitudes about diversity from his experience as a student, a faculty member, Board of Trustees secretary, chair of the Board, and general counsel, found Holbrook's efforts in this area admirable. "She never backed off on promoting diversity," he said, and "she insisted that women and minorities be included in all job searches." Board chair Longaberger agreed, observing that Holbrook's most important decision was to broaden a commitment to diversity, specifically the extension of benefits to sponsored dependents, which "effectively achieved an extension of basic benefits for the entire university community that had been a goal of several previous administrations and a longtime desire of the faculty, staff, and students."

The benefits extension was the result of a true partnership between the President and the chair of the Board working together on something that had gone without resolution for a long time. Assessing her more generally, Karen Bell, dean of the College of Arts during Holbrook's term, said she "loved working with her and appreciated her 'feminine' running of the university—she worked toward consensus, credited others (probably to a fault) for all the good work that went on, and worked towards the common good."

Verdicts on Holbrook's concern for diversity are uniformly positive, and Vice Provost and Special Assistant to the President for Diversity Mac Stewart seems to have best summarized that view. In 2006, noting Holbrook's decision to retire, Stewart said,

> [S]he is leaving us with a solid foundation on which to continue building. During her tenure, we experienced strong support and enhance-

ment of our diversity programs. Recruitment and retention efforts were intensified, especially in the wake of the recent Supreme Court ruling, and the president herself made phone calls to undecided minority recruits. New centers were opened—The Todd Bell Center for the African American Male—and existing ones like The Women's Place and Multicultural Center were given more appropriate space and greater visibility. The President and Provost's Diversity Lecture Series was broadened to include artistic performances so that we might experience, as well as hear about, different cultures. And the university named its first ever diversity officer.

The year 2006 was also when Holbrook served as grand marshal in the annual Columbus gay pride parade. Holbrook expressed her own commitment to diversity in language as strong: "Diversity is a value, and for Ohio State, achieving diversity among our population of students, faculty and staff is a goal. It is about fairness and justice to provide access to education for all citizens, and it is essential to prepare for life in the working world, for good citizenship, and for political leadership."

6

Reaching Out

Since our founding in 1870 as a land grant college, Ohio State has
proudly and effectively served Ohio and its people—educating hundreds
of thousands of Ohioans and applying our base of knowledge and skills
to economic and societal needs. Our proactive outreach and engagement
initiatives integrate teaching, scholarship, and research.
—*The Academic Plan*

Among the many demands placed on it by all kinds of people and organizations, one stands out above all others: Ohio State's foundational mission as a
land-grant university, which from its inception entailed the charge to serve
the citizenry of Ohio and the world, a charge with varying interpretations
that seems more crucial with each passing year. So it might go without saying
that during Holbrook's term, OSU would continue to widen its already broad
portfolio of programs aimed at serving the larger community. Holbrook,
however, put a distinctive stamp on this activity, frequently invoking the core
value enshrined in the Academic Plan that promised to "expand the land-
grant mission to address our society's compelling national needs." She also
had in mind two of the Plan's strategies—"develop academic programs that
define Ohio State as the nation's leading public land-grant university" and
"help build Ohio's future."

Prior to coming to OSU, Holbrook had held positions at more land-grant
universities (Wisconsin, Florida, and Georgia) than any of her predecessors,
and that long familiarity with them no doubt underlay her instinctive commitment to the central tenets of land-grant universities and the historic value
of their public work. Her developing agenda at OSU, which was shaped by an

attention to research, inevitably also underscored the importance of working with collaborating partners off campus and to produce, out of that research, expertise, ideas, and goods for communities beyond the campus.

An inventory of outreach/engagement activity during Holbrook's years might best begin with what occurred closer to campus and then move farther outward into myriad other communities. At the start of such a list would be the Service-Learning Initiative, which through courses offered in various colleges lets students be part of experiences that "connect service to the community with the learning objectives of the course." Holbrook defined service-learning in this way: it is "a key teaching and learning strategy that gives life and depth to the knowledge students acquire; helps them learn to use their knowledge to solve real problems that affect people's lives; gives them the experience and people skills they will need to make a difference. And it is one of the many ways our faculty and students make significant contributions as active members of our community."

A faculty roundtable, started in 1998 (and revised in 2001) by Vice Provost Garland, was established to oversee such courses, recommend funding of them, maintain a forum for evaluation of them, recognize faculty doing service-learning, and spread the word that service-learning is an ideal expression of the land-grant ethos. More than any other instructional form and as an instrument of the land-grant model, service-learning ideally makes students both learners and practical contributors. After they graduate, students might well work in those environments, but through service-learning programs they can also work there while still in school. Such initiatives have included the Human Ecology House in the University District, which offered student-supported social services for the neighborhood, and a course for Spanish majors developed by the Department of Spanish and Portuguese that directed students to human service centers that cater to Spanish speakers and improved students' language skills while they interpreted services for clients.

One of the most widely recognized examples of university outreach anywhere is the Metro Early College High School, a new Columbus public high school co-created by OSU, Battelle, and the Educational Council of Columbus-area schools, opened in 2006. Adjacent to the southwest corner of the OSU Columbus campus, Metro was designed as an academy devoted to the innovative teaching of mathematics, science, and technology. OSU faculty from the colleges of Education and Human Ecology, Mathematical and Physical Sciences, and Biological Sciences collaborated with the Metro High School staff to plan a curriculum meant to educate students in these areas of knowledge critical to national needs. The school was planned to start off and remain small, with enrollment capped at 400. As Holbrook said—and she was the driving spirit behind the project—the collaborative purpose in starting Metro was both to "increase the pool of well-prepared students applying to Ohio State and colleges in general but also to stimulate public-private partnerships elsewhere that might attract students back to science and mathematics." Metro was a contemporary echo of the University School, OSU's College of Education lab school that closed in the 1960s, but it differed in its significant STEM emphasis, its cooperative designing, and its explicit presidential patronage.

Also across the street from OSU was Metro's other partner, Battelle, the largest independent research and development organization in the world, which before and since but especially during Holbrook's time has been a major outreach partner of the university. The range of its always growing list of projects pursued jointly with OSU is best summarized in the 2007 North Central University accreditation report, *Time and Change*, which recounted the extensive cooperation this way:

> Ohio State-Battelle-shared facilities and research collaborations have grown among faculty in the Colleges of Food, Agricultural, and Environmental Sciences; Arts; Business; Education and Human Ecology; Engineering; Mathematical and Physical Sciences; Medicine; and Veterinary Medicine. Joint research includes the study of fuel cells, bioproducts, and cardiovascular and cancer therapies, as well as efforts in joint recruiting, public policy development, product innovation, entrepreneurship, and improving STEM education.

In 2006, the Federation of the Colleges of Arts and Sciences, imitating the more varied aims of the far-flung Ohio State University Extension, created an outreach and engagement office to link those colleges' vast academic resources with off-campus communities. According to Mindy Wright, then of the Arts and Sciences Colleges office, starting in 2006 it worked to devise ways of allowing high school students to earn college credit, through its ASC Nonprofit Advisory Committee, and to bring together students and faculty for service-learning courses and internships. In 2006, WOSU Public Media also created an outreach and engagement office and made headlines with its novel installation downtown at the Center of Science and Industry (COSI), where the museum and its partner broadcasting station together offered the public a media center, meeting space, exhibit area, and television and radio studios.

In a different sort of outreach into the Columbus community, OSU and the College of Arts, with Holbrook's endorsement, combined energies to carve out the new Urban Arts Space (UAS) downtown, an act that, on the one hand, answered the city's wish for OSU to be physically more visible in (and help grow) an incipient downtown culture and entertainment district and, on the other hand, offered the College of Arts a bigger presence in and a bridge to the wider community. Opened in February 2008, shortly after Holbrook's departure from OSU, the UAS and its exhibition space became a home for visual and performance art, an "arts laboratory" for student, faculty, alumni, and visiting and community artists. As then Dean of Arts Karen Bell recalls, "When it seemed that some city leaders were going to let go of the idea of an urban arts space, I asked Karen if I should continue to pursue it or let it go, and she said 'make it happen'—and we did."

OSU has also been accustomed to investing in the community for broader social purposes. Discussions between the university and the city of Columbus and, in particular, between Holbrook and Mayor Michael Coleman, led in 2004 to their announced intention to establish a new safety center southeast of campus and to splitting the $4.4 million cost of the center. Construction on the facility began in Holbrook's last year, and it opened the next year. It was intended to serve both the University District adjacent to campus and the Weinland Park neighborhood, and it houses a station with police officers from Precinct 4 and the OSU Public Safety Department, space for the Community Crime Patrol, the Neighborhood Pride Center, and meeting rooms for local residents.

The university made other, grander investments in the University District as well, and in collaboration with the city of Columbus. To foster urban revitalization in this area, OSU under Gordon Gee in 1995 had created Campus Partners for Community Urban Redevelopment; the city approved the Partners' revitalization plan two years later. In 2004, Holbrook helped break ground on construction of the mixed-use project along High Street called South Campus Gateway, and it opened in 2005. At the same time, the university began playing a critical role in the redevelopment of Weinland Park, which Stephen Sterrett, community relations director of Campus Partners, has described as a neighborhood of "concentrated poverty, deteriorated housing, instability, and crime." Following buy-in from various city and university stakeholders, in 2007 Holbrook presided over inauguration of the new Weinland Park Elementary School and an accompanying education laboratory, the Schoenbaum Family Center. Gateway became a model for other urban universities and a working example of town-gown cooperation.

Perhaps most emblematic of the university's and Holbrook's commitment to science and technology—and to the fruits of research in those areas that benefit society—was their continued support for the Science and Technology

Campus Corporation, or SciTech, the regional initiative located on OSU's West Campus that hosted cooperative development projects and research sponsorships, bringing together faculty, businesses, and entrepreneurs. Begun in 1997, SciTech belonged to the umbrella organization TechColumbus. And of course the expanding Ohio State Medical Center not only attracted an ever-widening community of patients but, in the words of medical historian Dr. George Paulson, "a proliferation of specialty and operative areas outside the OSU hospital." In 2006, Holbrook and the Board of Trustees approved construction of a biomedical research tower meant to house the increasingly prominent medical and scientific researchers whose work would serve everyone.

All of these OSU outreach and engagement efforts during the Holbrook years illustrate the ways that academic knowledge can improve the lives of all citizens, both on and off campus. Holbrook's clear belief in the land-grant mandate to reach out was a telling feature of her term.

7

Departure and Confluence

> We are looking for a man of fine appearance, of commanding presence, one who will impress the public; he must be a fine speaker at public assemblies; he must be a great scholar and a great teacher; he must be a preacher also, as some think; he must be a man of winning manners; he must have tact so that he can get along with and govern the faculty; he must be popular with the students; he must also be a man of business training, a man of affairs; he must be a great administrator. Gentlemen, there is no such man.
> —*U.S. President and later OSU Board of Trustees member Rutherford B. Hayes, to the Board during a search for a new president, 1894*

In July 2005, Karen Holbrook and the Board of Trustees agreed to postpone for a year any negotiation about her possible reappointment. Then, nearly a year later, on May 31, 2006, she asked the Board to accept her decision to retire from the presidency at the conclusion of her five-year contract, on June 30, 2007. She said her decision was informed mainly by a desire to spend more time with her husband, Jim, and by her belief that the university should have a president who was able to make the multi-year commitment needed to lead its next capital campaign.

From the beginning of her term and increasingly as its end approached— and as her successes and challenges started to come more sharply into relief— observers were reminded of the reasons that she and Ohio State chose each other back in 2002. Like the other presidents since Harold Enarson, she had had a lengthy career as a productive faculty member at comparable universities (two of them OSU benchmark institutions). She was also a scientist with strong professional credentials both as a researcher and as a research administrator who helped faculty and programs acquire impressive levels of external research funding. In addition, as a cell biologist, she was especially familiar with developments and policy issues in medical science, a familiarity valuable for the president of a university with a major medical center. All of her profile—plus, as then Board chair Jim Patterson put it, the Board's belief in "her ability to relate to other people"—led to her selection.

Now, as the end of a term approached, various observers began to evaluate her according to what seemed to be at least four measures: how well she had deployed her experience, how successfully she had demonstrated her political skills, how engaging had been her personal style, and how generally people had viewed her decisions and actions. It is a truism that we too often set impossible standards for university presidents and, at least since the time of Rutherford B. Hayes, that we as often tend to judge them either too harshly or too effusively, but judgments are unavoidable.

As for her experience: Some of her harsher critics (mostly later in her term) thought that if she had previously been a president at a university like OSU she might have worked better with the Board of Trustees. She had supporters and critics among its changing membership, strong supporters like Jim Patterson and Tami Longaberger, but also some Trustees who wished she had had presidential experience. Nevertheless, all agreed that her career as a researcher and research manager constituted a big advantage for the university, as did her prominent membership on boards of prestigious academic organizations, all of which only helped OSU as it rose in the rankings—the Association of American Universities, the National Association of State Universities and Land-Grant Colleges, the American Council on Education, the American Association for the Advancement of Science, and the Association of American Medical Colleges. In fact, it seemed natural that, after leaving OSU, she would return to overseeing a university research program (as vice president for research and innovation at the University of South Florida), whereas the three preceding OSU presidents, upon finishing their terms, assumed a chancellorship (Kirwan), another presidency (Gee), or another university administrative role (Jennings). Holbrook's life has been research.

As for political skills: Some wished she had been more adept at media relations and at managing her public image, matters that someone who had previously held a presidency might have handled more successfully, and others wished she had connected better with the wider Columbus community and the Ohio legislature. But she earned more than passing grades for her astute handling of sensational events that caught the media's attention and required hers, early and late in her term—uncivil football game-day behavior, football star Maurice Clarett's allegations, the murders and other deaths of students, the firing of a basketball coach, and overseeing debates about the treatment of laboratory chimpanzees. And in the midst of some of these more public dramas, her mother died shortly after they both moved to Columbus.

As for her personal style: Some wished she were more of an extrovert who delighted in large crowds and in more frequent receptions for university friends and supporters, readying OSU for the rigors of the next major fundraising campaign (although her average of twenty-eight events a year held at the President's Residence in Bexley was not that much less than Brit Kirwan's thirty-three). But others found her to be highly engaging when in intense conversations with small groups; and in each of her five years, total private support averaged a healthy $204,500,000. She may have preferred to avoid confrontation, but decisions like the tailgate restrictions showed her to be a leader of conviction. She may have been thought by some to be reticent about seeking or taking others' advice, but she definitely was confident of her own opinion, often emphasizing the primacy of her own judgment in making decisions. Like many a leader, she seemed to some as too hands-on and detail-occupied, known, for instance, for keeping her own files, drafting and revising her own speeches, and maintaining an office calendar that was unstrategically open to all who sought her attention. But at the same time, such personalized communication made her distinctive as a president; and what one viewer might see as too hands-on another might see as the typical labors of a self-professed workaholic (see in the Appendix [A.14] her weekly calendar from 2002 and 2007).

Regarding a last category of activity—decisions and actions: While some would criticize her for not doing more to exert greater fiscal discipline and governance over the Medical Center and alignment between it and the rest of the university, some of those same critics would applaud her unwavering decision to suppress the mayhem that had come to surround football games. And a simple listing of the decisions she made and actions she took related to but one sphere of academic activity—research—would amount to a portfolio of achievement that any university leader would envy: creating the Honors Collegium, Scholars, and the Undergraduate Research office; expanding the Denman Forum; establishing the Urban Arts Space and the Kirwan Institute for the Study of Race and Ethnicity; beginning reforms of the Graduate School; determining to renovate the Thompson Library; instituting the research faculty rank; approving the Biomedical Research Tower; directing the faculty in their competition for the governor's Third Frontier funding; and devising with her provost the Targeted Investment in Excellence program—not to mention other research-related projects like the Metro School, freshman seminars, and interdisciplinary majors. Her term was full of decisions, and inactive she wasn't.

The chair of the Board who hired her, Jim Patterson, has offered this positive view of her achievements: "During Karen Holbrook's tenure, every measurement of excellence that signifies a great university reached new heights—the amount of research dollars, the retention rates of students, the graduation rate, the amount of the endowment, the academic excellence of entering freshmen, to name just a few. Under her leadership, Ohio State continued on its path to eminence as one of the world's finest universities."

As she finished her term, Board member Brian Hicks remarked that she had accomplished plenty of importance and that "people are going to know that impact after she's gone." As someone who many of her coworkers found to be humble in describing her own accomplishments and modest about taking credit for them, Holbrook probably would want to qualify Hicks's statement. She might well instead use a different term to characterize what she tried to do over the five years—*confluence,* a term that seemed important in her thinking and a notion that had two meanings for her. Sometimes she used it to describe the ways that a particular element of the university's academic mission—research, say—could become a unifying common denominator across many arenas of the university (in the case of research, from the undergraduate curriculum to faculty scholarship to OSU extension and community engagement). Confluence also meant for her the way that the actions of several presidents flow together over time to affect accomplishments that then belong to no one of them but to all of them collectively. As she explains in "Fixing the Fragmented University," she is keenly aware of something that former dean John Mount often underscores, namely, that many of the accomplishments attributed to her had their roots in the decisions and actions of predecessors, just as much of what she started would be finished by her successors. The Academic Plan, she liked to say, was "a source of confluence." In the same way, campus buildings get approved by one administration, designed during the next one, and inaugurated by still another. Similarly, Holbrook's decision ultimately to create a Federation of the Arts and Sciences came out of years of discussion, and Arts and Sciences would not finally become a single, unified college until sometime later. Holbrook's appreciation of this confluence over time is nicely emphasized in the university's 2007 reaccreditation report, authorized by her, titled *Time and Change:* "Through the terms of three University presidents—E. Gordon Gee (1990–1998), William E. Kirwan (1998–2002), and Karen A. Holbrook (2002–2007)—and three provosts—Richard J. Sisson (1993–1998), Edward J. Ray (1998–2003), and Barbara R. Snyder (2003–2007)—the University has undertaken a set of institution-wide initiatives related to the internal goal of continuously improving, and thus strengthening, the various components of its academic mission." Actions, in other words, are more likely confluential than individual, especially those of presidents, and credit is collaborative.

For the three months between the end of Holbrook's term and the return of Gordon Gee to the president's office, Interim Executive Vice President and Provost Joe Alutto served as interim president. Holbrook became a finalist for president at Florida Gulf Coast University but then took a vice president position at the University of South Florida, which she still holds, not far from her and her husband Jim's Florida home on Longboat Key. She made a first visit back to Ohio State in April 2008 for the dedication of the new LEED-certified Nationwide and Ohio Farm Bureau 4-H Center, a building she had approved years before. The audience that welcomed her back that day would continue to realize, along with the rest of us, that, like the presidents who came before her, she in a sense never really left.

With Vice President for Student Affairs William Hall at the spring 2005 commencement.
Source: The *Columbus Dispatch* Photo Archives.

Testifying in the 2005 trial of head basketball coach Jim O'Brien, who had sued OSU for breach of contract in his firing. Source: The *Columbus Dispatch* Photo Archives.

With Arizona senator John S. McCain, following his address at the spring 2006 commencement. Source: The *Columbus Dispatch* Photo Archives.

With benefactor John F. Wolfe, recognizing Tierra Poindexter, a student recipient, at the 2006 Wolfe Scholarship Dinner. Source: OSU Photo Services.

With Director of Libraries Joseph Branin and Athletics Director Gene Smith in 2006, acknowledging the Athletics donation to the Library renovation. Source: OSU Photo Services.

During an interview in spring 2007. Source: The *Columbus Dispatch* Photo Archives.

With Trustee Karen Hendricks and Athletics Director Andy Geiger at the 2006 dedication of the Steelwood Athletic Facility. Source: OSU Photo Services.

Leading participation in community service at a Phoenix food bank preceding the 2006 National Championship football game. Source: OSU Photo Services.

Greeting Provost Barbara Snyder at a 2007 farewell reception for the President. Source: OSU Photo Services.

Surprised by induction into Sphinx Senior Honorary at a spring 2007 Board of Trustees meeting. Source: OSU Photo Services.

With former senator John Glenn and Provost Snyder at the 2007 Kiplinger Dinner. Source: OSU Photo Services.

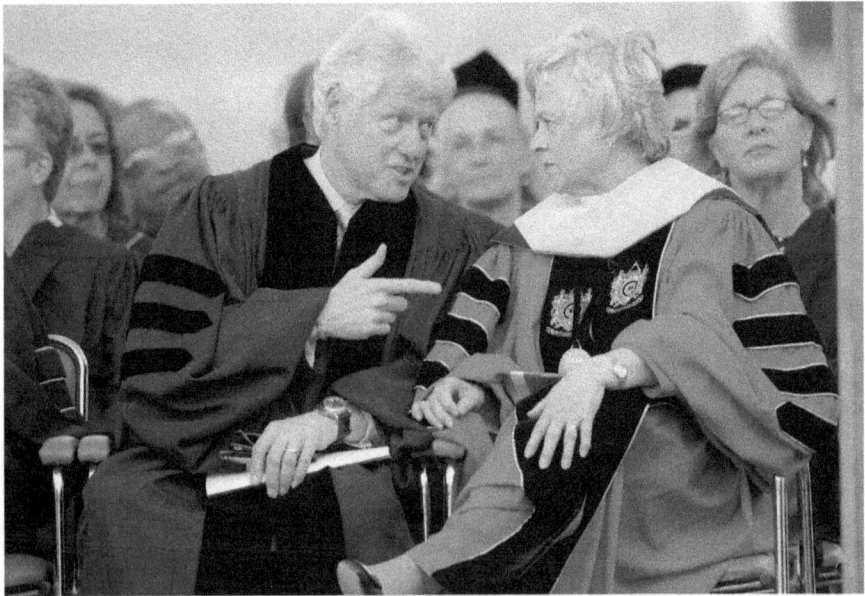

Exchanging views following former president Bill Clinton's spring 2007 commencement address. Source: The *Columbus Dispatch* Photo Archives.

Singing "Carmen Ohio" at the farewell reception. Source: OSU Photo Services.

Appendix

A.1. Amended Establishment and Appointment of Presidential Search Committee

Resolution No. 2002-101

Synopsis: Establishment and appointment of Presidential Search Committee is proposed.

WHEREAS Dr. William E. Kirwan has announced his decision to relinquish the presidency of The Ohio State University in order to assume the chancellorship of the University System of Maryland; and

WHEREAS it is the responsibility of the Board of Trustees, pursuant to section 3335.09 of the Ohio Revised Code, to select the President of the University; and

WHEREAS the Board of Trustees has determined that it is appropriate to establish and appoint a Search Committee with broad representation of University constituencies and charge it with responsibility for recommending to the Board one or more candidates to be the next President of the University; and

WHEREAS in order to proceed expeditiously with the commencement of the search it is appropriate to constitute and give an initial charge to the Search Committee:

NOW THEREFORE BE IT RESOLVED, That the Search Committee for President of The Ohio State University will have the following membership:

Trustees

      James F. Patterson, Chair

      Robert M. Duncan

      Karen L. Hendricks

      Dimon R. McFerson

Members of the Faculty

      Bruce E. Bursten, Professor, Department of Chemistry

      Susan Fisher, Professor, Department of Entomology/Secretary
         of the University Senate

      David O. Frantz, Professor, Department of English

      Jacqueline J. Royster, Professor, Departments of English and
         African-American and African Studies/Associate Dean,
         College of Humanities

      Marilynn Brewer, Professor, Department of Psychology

Deans

      Fred Sanfilippo, Senior Vice President for Health Sciences/
         Dean of the College of Medicine and Public Health

      James C. Williams, Dean, College of Engineering

Students

      Edward Pauline, President, Undergraduate Student Government

      Marsha R. Robinson, Graduate Student, Ph.D. candidate in
         History

      Professional Student to be named

Administrators

      Jerry A. May, Vice President for Development/President of
         the University Foundation

      Mac A. Stewart, Vice Provost for Minority Affairs

Alumni Association representative

      Dan L. Heinlen, President and CEO, Alumni Association

Non-Teaching Staff

      Willa Young, Chair, Staff Advisory Council

BE IT FURTHER RESOLVED, That James F. Patterson shall serve as Chair of the Search Committee and that the following people will serve the Board and Committee as follows: William J. Napier, liaison; Virginia M. Trethewey, general counsel; and Mary A. Basinger, administrative coordinator; and

BE IT FURTHER RESOLVED, That each member of the Search Committee shall commit herself or himself to representing the best interests of the University in planning and directing all aspects of a comprehensive and expeditious search for a new President including, but not limited to, developing a profile of characteristics, skills and qualities desired in the next president; developing a list of candidates and verifying their qualifications, availability and interest in the position; and making a recommendation of one or more candidates to the Board; and

BE IT FURTHER RESOLVED, That the Chair of the Search Committee shall provide periodic updates to the Board of Trustees at its regularly scheduled meetings until the search is concluded; and

BE IT FURTHER RESOLVED, That the Search Committee shall serve until discharged by the Board of Trustees or upon the appointment of a new President; and

BE IT FURTHER RESOLVED, That any actions taken by the Search Committee or the Chair in furtherance of this Resolution prior to its effective date are hereby ratified and approved.

Upon motion of Judge Duncan, seconded by Ms. Hendricks, the Board of Trustees adopted the foregoing resolution by unanimous roll call vote, cast by Messrs. Brennan, Patterson, Sofia, Slane, McFerson, and Judge Duncan, Mses. Longaberger, Hendricks, and Davidson.

A.2. Chronology of the 2002 Presidential Search

Monday, March 25 — Dr. William E. Kirwan announces that he will leave Ohio State to become Chancellor of the University System of Maryland.

Friday, April 5 — Board of Trustees establish and appoint an 18-member Presidential Search Committee (resolution attached) to seek a successor to Dr. William E. Kirwan. Members are:

Faculty:	Bruce Bursten, Susan Fisher, David Frantz, Jackie Royster, Marilynn Brewer
Deans:	Fred Sanfilippo, Jim Williams
Students:	Eddie Pauline, Marsha Robinson, Soraya Rofagha
Administrators:	Jerry May, Mac Stewart
Alumni:	Dan Heinlen
Staff:	Willa Young

Letters of appointment sent to committee. Website on the search established.

Thursday, April 11 — Chairman Patterson and a few search committee members begin talking to university and community leaders (list attached) with regard to expectations of the next president.

Full search committee meets for first time over dinner with President Kirwan to hear "What are the Dimensions, Roles, and Responsibilities of the President of The Ohio State University?"

Friday, April 12 — Search committee meets and discusses confidentiality, search firm selection, and presidential profile. Notebook distributed to the members that includes:
- Office of Human Resources, *A Guide to Effective Searches*
- 1997 Presidential Search: A Review and Chronology
- Profile of the President of The Ohio State University
- Presidential Search Committee Roster

- Board of Trustees 2001-2002 Roster
- Search Committee Operating Protocol

The committee also hears from:
- Herb Asher, counselor to the president, "What can we learn from the past? What should we look for in the future?"
- Alex Shumate, chair of the 1997 search committee, "Last time – What went right? What went wrong?"

Friday, April 19 — Search committee meets and receives input from provost; vice provost for minority affairs; vice presidents for university development, student affairs, and research, and past and present Alumni Association presidents.

Wednesday, April 24 — Subcommittee to review search firms begins task. Members are: Bob Duncan, Karen Hendricks, Dimon McFerson, Marsha Robinson, Jackie Royster, and Ginny Trethewey (ex-officio).

Tuesday, April 25 — Subgroup of search committee travels to Washington, D.C. to talk with presidents of the American Association of Universities, American Council on Education, and the National Association of State Universities and Land-Grant Colleges.

Wednesday, April 26 — Jim Patterson and Bob Duncan visit with Governor.

Search committee meets and receives update from Chairman on meetings with community leaders, et al. Group also hears from senior vice president for health sciences/dean of the college of medicine and public health; academic medical center leadership; executive deans; chair of diversity council; director of athletics; faculty leadership; and student leadership.

Monday, April 29 — Open Forum with university community. Panel made up of several search committee members, led by Trustee Duncan.

Tuesday, April 30   Search firm subcommittee reviews five proposals. Bids received from: A.T. Kearney (Jan Greenwood); Hudepohl & Assoc.; Heidrick & Struggles.

Thursday, May 2   Two search firm candidates interviewed by subcommittee. Chairman Patterson and selected search committee members continue to discuss expectations with community leaders.

Friday, May 3   First report on search committee's progress given at University Board meeting by Chairman Jim Patterson.

Search Committee meets and hears from vice president for business and finance; ag leadership; chair of university staff advisory committee; and faculty representatives for the advisory committee to the vice president for research.

Monday, May 6   Second Open Form held. Panel made up of several search committee members, led by Chairman Patterson.

Thursday, May 9   Search firm announced: A.T. Kearney, Inc.

Friday, May 10   Search committee meets to discuss presidential profile. Bernie Erven, faculty member in ag, serves as moderator to help develop profile. Search firm representatives join in by conference call. Two search committee members appointed to take results and develop a draft profile.

Thursday, May 16   Search committee meets with A.T. Kearney representatives to discuss next steps.

Friday, May 17   Ad for position approved for submission in: *Chronicle of Higher Education, Black Issues in Higher Education, Women in Higher Education, University Posting,* and *HigherEd.com* website (through Human Resources).

Friday, June 7   Search firm selection of A.T. Kearney approved. Presidential

Profile (attached) also approved at Board of Trustees meeting, and Chairman Jim Patterson gives update on search.

Dr. Ed Jennings is appointed interim-president.

Monday, June 10–12   Representative group of search committee meets in D.C. for discussions with possible candidates.

Monday, June 17   Representative group of search committee meets in D.C. for discussions with possible candidates.

Thursday, June 20   Chairman Patterson holds conference call with the search committee members who traveled to D.C. to review and discuss potential candidates.

Friday, June 21   Chairman Patterson holds conference call with entire search committee to update them on progress of search.

Wednesday, June 26   Representative group of search committee meets in D.C. for discussions with possible candidates.

Tuesday, July 2   Representative group of search committee meets in D.C. for discussions with possible candidates.

Chairman Patterson appoints a subcommittee of two trustees to develop compensation package. They are: Zuheir Sofia and Tami Longaberger.

Sunday, July 7–18   Interviews and discussions with potential candidates continue.

Wednesday, July 24   News release sent out announcing special Board meeting.

Thursday, July 25   Trustees announce, approve, and present Dr. Karen Holbrook as Ohio State's Thirteenth President. Lunch follows with trustees, search committee members, cabinet, deans, student leaders, and special guests.

Tuesday, October 1   President Holbrook takes office.

A.3. Academic Plan: Executive Summary

The Ohio State University aspires to be among the world's truly great universities—advancing the well-being of the people of Ohio and the global community through the creation and dissemination of knowledge. Ohio needs a great teaching and research university for a rich flow of ideas, innovation, and graduates from a wide variety of disciplines. Ohio also needs a great university to be what *The New York Times* has called a "revving economic engine" that spurs strategic growth in the new Information Age economy.

Any review of the comparative data makes it clear that our focus must be on building academic excellence. For while the University needs to continuously improve in many areas, we will never be a great university without dramatically enhancing the reality and perception of our teaching and learning as well as our research and scholarship—and without enhancing the service activities that flow from our excellence in these endeavors.

Over recent years, we have focused on four core elements: Becoming a national leader in the quality of our academic programs; being universally recognized for the quality of the learning experience we offer our students; creating an environment that truly values and is enriched by diversity; and expanding the land-grant mission to address our society's most compelling needs.

These core elements are reflected in the six strategies and fourteen supporting initiatives that follow. While the University will undertake many more initiatives over the next five years, these are considered the most transformational.

STRATEGY: BUILD A WORLD-CLASS FACULTY

1. Over the next three to five years, recruit at least twelve faculty members who have attained or have the potential to attain the highest honors in their disciplines, concentrating these appointments in areas of strategic focus.

2. Implement a faculty recruitment, retention, and development plan—including a competitive, merit-based compensation structure—that is in line with our peer institutions.

STRATEGY: DEVELOP ACADEMIC PROGRAMS THAT DEFINE OHIO STATE AS THE NATION'S LEADING PUBLIC LAND-GRANT UNIVERSITY

3. Continue the Strategic Investment approach by competitively funding initiatives that build programmatic strength and open new fields. Build on existing capabilities and capture opportunities specific to Ohio State and to Ohio. Maintain ongoing multidisciplinary initiatives where appropriate and develop new initiatives that draw on University-wide strengths to attack major problems of the next quarter century. Create multidisciplinary centers that can attract additional faculty in key areas, helping reduce student-faculty ratios in high-demand fields.

4. Significantly increase space dedicated to funded research beyond what is currently planned. Include a multidisciplinary building devoted to high-quality research space as well as to office and meeting space.

STRATEGY: ENHANCE THE QUALITY OF THE TEACHING AND LEARNING ENVIRONMENT

5. Transform the Library into a twenty-first century Information Age center within the next five to ten years.

6. Upgrade the quality of our classroom pool space and enhance the appearance of the campus facilities and grounds.

7. Provide faculty, staff, and students with the latest technology tools for leadership in teaching, research, and career development within the next five years.

STRATEGY: ENHANCE AND BETTER SERVE THE STUDENT BODY

8. Within the next three years, make admissions to Ohio State selective throughout the year for new freshmen and for all transfer students.

9. Create a rich educational environment for undergraduates. Increase course accessibility, reduce class sizes, and establish at least ten scholars programs within five years—expanding opportunities for students to live with those who share common interests and enhancing students' academic success and sense of community. Provide academic programming, advising, and career counseling within these communities.

10. Provide ample need-based and merit-based aid for undergraduates and a competitive financial aid and fellowship support package for graduate and professional students to improve Ohio State's graduate and professional matriculation rate.

STRATEGY: CREATE A DIVERSE UNIVERSITY COMMUNITY

11. Hire at least five to ten women and five to ten minority faculty at a senior level each year for five years through the Faculty Hiring Assistance Program (FHAP) and other initiatives.

12. Recruit, support, and retain to graduation larger numbers of academically able minority students.

STRATEGY: HELP BUILD OHIO'S FUTURE

13. Significantly strengthen the scope and effectiveness of our commitment to P-12 public education, with a special focus on the education of underserved children and youth. In so doing, work with the State of Ohio and selected local school districts. This initiative will be a University-wide partnership, with the College of Education in the lead college role.

14. Become the catalyst for the development of Ohio's technology-based economy. Increase collaborations with the private sector to enhance research, successfully transfer University technology, and provide experiential learning and career opportunities for students.

To successfully implement this ambitious agenda, the University must take four Facilitating Actions: Obtain increased state support, improve the organization and delivery of instruction, increase organizational flexibility, and improve the faculty work environment. The Plan identifies specific steps to meet these needs.

Over the next five years, the University expects to invest in the range of $750 million in new and reallocated resources to implement this plan, with spending scaled up or down depending upon actual funding. The Plan identifies potential sources for the needed revenues. A set of strategic indicators will help measure our progress.

A.4. Leadership Agenda

November 18, 2004

This Leadership Agenda provides the specific priorities under the Academic Plan for action and resource allocation, guided by consultation with academic, administrative, faculty, staff, and student leadership. Our overarching goal, as identified in the Academic Plan, is to be one of the world's truly great research universities. That goal will be reached only by prioritizing our actions and focusing on those that are most likely to improve our reputation and our performance in the context of fiscal responsibility.

To facilitate achievement of this Leadership Agenda and our aspirations of academic excellence, the University must move rapidly toward a more dynamic and constructive culture, identifying and building on our strengths and rejecting limiting behaviors. The foundational elements of this culture are creativity, high performance, and commitment, as highlighted below.

Creativity flourishes in a dynamic environment that encourages risk-taking, seeks and values ideas from all, and requires visionary and inspirational leadership. Leaders are responsible for creating an environment that nurtures creativity.

High performance is expected in an environment of accountability and transparency, which includes the ability to set and act on priorities. A high-performance culture drives out entitlements and mediocrity; utilizes incentives and awards; values diversity; fosters synergy from collaborations across units; and flows from strategic planning that is informed by data, knowledge, and experience and guided by metrics.

Commitment to performance is strengthened by an aspiration to have a more dynamic culture by creating an environment which fully engages all, instills institutional pride, and treats each person with respect and dignity; and by ensuring that all program priorities ultimately benefit the University as a whole and society. This cultural transformation will require our full and passionate participation.

The initiatives in the three areas of focus—distinctive education for students, cutting-edge interdisciplinary research, and 21st-century outreach and engagement—are heavily intertwined. Together these initiatives are designed to increase the quality of education for our students, the academic excellence and national prestige of our university, and the economic impact of our research and outreach activities. The objectives described in the Leadership Agenda complement the high priority that the University places on accountability to our stakeholders, access and affordability for students, and recruitment and retention of the best faculty and staff. Continued support for student scholarships and competitive compensation for faculty and staff are essential for success.

The University's leadership team has initiated action on each of the items listed below. We expect to report annually on progress in each area.

Use of Leadership Agenda in Organizational Unit Planning

The core values and strategies articulated in the Academic Plan provide a broad context for academic plans developed by colleges, departments, and academic support units. Correspondingly, the annual goals and actions established in the annual Leadership Agenda should be incorporated on an annual basis into the evolving action plans at the unit level. As college and department leaders work with faculty, staff, and other stakeholders in the revising of their units' plans, these planning activities should occur with full knowledge and understanding by all participants of the context provided by the Academic Plan, and also the more specific goals and actions described in the annual Leadership Agenda. Each unit should incorporate and integrate, as appropriate, the Leadership Agenda goals into its respective plan and strive to support and achieve those goals through actions performed both within the unit and through collaboration with other organizations internal and external to the campus. Finally, performance metrics must be established at each administrative level to measure on a continuing basis success in accomplishing stated actions, and thereby assess the progress toward achieving the goals.

I. DISTINCTIVE EDUCATIONAL EXPERIENCES AND OPPORTUNITIES FOR STUDENTS

One strategy identified in the Academic Plan is to enhance and better serve the student body. In the core values, we stated that we want to "ignite a lifelong love of learning" and "open the world to our students." Ohio State's breadth and depth allow us to attract top students and offer them distinctive educational experiences and opportunities. We want every student to leave Ohio State with a

APPENDIX

degree, a sense of intellectual accomplishment and cultural curiosity, a lifelong engagement with learning, and having had direct and significant interactions with faculty members. To enhance the education of undergraduate, graduate, and professional students, over the next two years we will take the following steps.

For undergraduate students, we will:

1. Recruit an entering freshman class with a median ACT score of 26 by 2006 (with a target of 27 by 2008). Continue to improve student retention.

Five hundred thousand dollars in new continuing funds was allocated in the FY 2005 budget process for strategic recruitment efforts designed to enhance the academic profile of the freshmen entering in fall 2005 and to attract students who will contribute to diversity on our campus. This is the first phase of the Ohio State 2008 Enrollment Management Plan.

responsibility center: Office of Academic Affairs (Offices of Undergraduate Studies and Admissions); Office of Student Affairs.

2. Review undergraduate education, including the General Education Curriculum and the total number of hours required for graduation, to create an undergraduate education that better reflects the quality of our students as well as university priorities such as diversity, research, interdisciplinarity, and outreach.

The university-wide committee to review undergraduate education will be appointed fall quarter 2004, with a report expected by June 2005.

responsibility center: Office of Academic Affairs; University Senate; Arts and Sciences Faculty Senate.

3. Create additional opportunities for greater interaction between faculty and undergraduate students including research experiences, mentoring programs, and seminars.

a. Colleges must now report on research opportunities for undergraduates. All colleges with undergraduate programs are offering undergraduate research experiences. The Office of Academic Affairs (Undergraduate Studies) and the Office of Research will collaborate to create an Office of Undergraduate Research, which will be responsible for 1) creating and maintaining a searchable database of faculty research interests to facilitate contacts between faculty and undergraduate students interested in research opportunities; 2) overseeing the Denman Undergraduate Research Forum; and 3) coordinating central support for undergraduate research. The Office of Undergraduate Research will be launched in FY 2006.

b. The Colleges of the Arts and Sciences assumed leadership of the President's freshman seminar initiative. Freshman seminars were offered for the first time in 2003–4, and the number of seminars offered will increase in 2004–5. The Colleges of the Arts and Sciences and the Council on Academic Affairs will review the two-year pilot program this year, and the university-wide committee to review undergraduate education will consider the role of freshman seminars in undergraduate education.

responsibility center: Offices of Academic Affairs (Undergraduate Studies) and Research; Council on Academic Affairs; departments, schools, and colleges.

4. Create additional novel undergraduate majors, minors, and courses that leverage the breadth of academic programs across the University.

These majors, minors, and courses will build on existing interdisciplinary academic offerings. We will also encourage the development of courses that include an international experience.

responsibility center: schools, colleges, departments; Office of Academic Affairs; Council on Academic Affairs.

For graduate and professional students, we will:

1. Examine doctoral programs to ensure that funding promotes quality.

The report from the Freeman Committee on Graduate Education is due on January 15, 2005. The report will be widely shared with groups across campus, including the Senate Fiscal Committee and the University Senate.

responsibility center: Office of Academic Affairs, deans, Graduate School.

2. Create new minors and interdisciplinary specializations for graduate and professional students.

The request for proposals was sent out by the Graduate School in October 2004.

responsibility center: Graduate School, in coordination with departments, schools, and colleges.

3. Develop the president's Interdisciplinary Seminar Series to bring together faculty and graduate and professional students from multiple disciplines to address issues of importance to Ohio, the nation, and the world.

Planning is underway in 2004–5 for the seminar series in 2005–6.

responsibility center: Graduate School, in coordination with the Office of Research and departments, schools, and colleges.

For all students, we will:

1. Through expanded recruitment and financial aid, as well as renewed efforts to improve the campus climate, enhance diversity to serve our educational mission.

a. In FY 2004, we allocated $500,000 in new continuing funds for the Morrill Scholarship Program. In fall 2003 we awarded Morrill Scholarship funds to 424 new freshmen, and for fall 2004 we awarded Morrill funds to 458 incoming freshmen. We allocated some additional funding for Graduate Enrichment Fellowships. We also allocated additional funds for enhanced recruitment efforts targeted to minority students. We will continue to monitor recruitment efforts designed to increase diversity on our campus.

b. Existing efforts to improve the campus climate for diversity, such as the President's and Provost's Diversity Lecture Series, will continue. We will also continue to work with the Senate Diversity Committee and the Diversity Council on issues related to the campus climate.

responsibility center: Office of Academic Affairs (Offices of Minority Affairs, Undergraduate Studies, Admissions, and Financial Aid); Senate Committee on Diversity; University Diversity Council; Office of Student Affairs.

2. Invest in technology to enrich faculty teaching and student learning.

Seventy-six percent of the tuition earmarked for learning technology went to the colleges. Central funds were used by the CIO to address three priorities: cybersecurity, which was improved with the installation in June 2004 of virus-blocking software to the central e-mail system; the learning environment, which was improved by installing hardware to create more "smart classrooms" in the central pool and by adding staff members to support faculty use of instructional technology, the development of instructional materials, and the classroom helpline; and web-based services to students, which were improved by the creation of an integrated website for student academic services such as registration, scheduling, course permissions and waitlists, grades, and a web-based degree-planning tool. During 2004–5, the Office of the CIO will begin work on the wireless project, which will create a centrally managed wireless network with access points in common areas, three wireless data frequency standards, and standard university-wide authentication and encryption, as well as continue to develop the course management system.

responsibility center: Office of the CIO, Office of Academic Affairs, colleges.

3. Make on-campus student housing that is safe and high-quality an institutional priority to enhance student academic achievement.

The April 27, 2004 housing plan, which calls for the conversion of Archer House, Fawcett Center, and Lincoln Tower to student housing, was recommended by the Offices of Student Affairs, Academic Affairs, and Business and Finance and was approved by President Holbrook. The conversion of Archer House and Fawcett Center should be completed by fall 2006. The Lincoln Tower conversion is more complex due to the number of offices involved; we anticipate student occupancy no earlier than fall 2008.

responsibility center: Office of Student Affairs; Office of Business and Finance.

II. CUTTING-EDGE INTERDISCIPLINARY RESEARCH FOR SHORT- AND LONG-TERM SOCIETAL BENEFITS

The Academic Plan calls for the development of academic programs that define Ohio State as the nation's leading public land-grant university. One of the core values identified in the Academic Plan is to "[p]roduce discoveries that make the world a better place." To achieve distinction as a research university, we must produce cutting-edge interdisciplinary scholarship that will provide short- and long-term benefits for society. To facilitate that research, during the next two years we will:

1. Fund the development of extramural grant proposals for large multidisciplinary centers by competitively awarding appropriate support.

Twenty excellent proposals were received from our faculty and reviewed by a select team of researchers from across the University. Based upon the recommendations of the selection committee, seven proposals were selected and awards were made on October 6, 2004. After implementation of program modifications suggested by the deans, the Large Interdisciplinary Seed Grant Program will again solicit proposals and will award seed grants during the 2004–5 academic year.

Recognizing that external funding for the large interdisciplinary centers is unavailable in some disciplines, the President and the Office of Research made available $500,000 for the Interdisciplinary Arts and Humanities Seed Grant competition. Grants were awarded in 2003–4, and the program was renewed for 2004–5. The request for proposals went out in November 2004.

responsibility center: Office of Research.

2. Support the development of interdisciplinary research institutes that bring together the most accomplished disciplinary and interdisciplinary scholars at the University. These institutes will attract leading scholars from other institutions, foster interdisciplinary research, and assist in communicating its impact. The institutes will also develop collaborations with public and private-sector partners and provide research opportunities for students.

responsibility center: Office of Research; departments, schools, and colleges.

3. Implement and effectively utilize a research faculty track.

Amendments to university rules approved by the Board of Trustees on June 4, 2004, allow tenure-initiating units to provide for the appointment of research faculty. Units planning to hire research faculty must first have an approved Appointments, Promotion, and Tenure document that specifies criteria for appointments, reappointments, and promotions. As of October 2004, two tenure-initiating units have A, P, and T documents that permit the hiring of research faculty.

responsibility center: Office of Academic Affairs, Office of Research, departments, schools, and colleges.

4. Identify and propose solutions to real and perceived procedural and/or financial barriers to progress in interdisciplinary research and teaching.

The Senate Fiscal Committee and the Ad Hoc Committee on Non-Fiscal Barriers to Interdisciplinarity have provided recommendations to the Offices of Academic Affairs and Business and Finance. In parallel, the Senior Vice President for Research has initiated discussions with the Office of Business and Finance, the Research Foundation, the college deans, and the directors of existing university research centers to ensure that departments and colleges receive adequate credit and fiscal reward for their participation in interdisciplinary efforts. The results of these discussions and the recommendations of the Senate Fiscal Committee and the Ad Hoc Committee will inform our implementation plan.

responsibility center: Offices of Academic Affairs, Business and Finance, and Research.

III. OUTREACH AND ENGAGEMENT INITIATIVES THAT CONNECT AREAS OF ACADEMIC EXCELLENCE WITH SOCIETAL NEEDS

Helping to build Ohio's future is another strategy in the Academic Plan. The vision statement asks Ohio State to "set the standard for the creation and dissemination of knowledge in service to its communities, state, nation, and the world." To put that vision into operation, our outreach and engagement initiatives must connect Ohio State's areas of academic excellence with societal needs. Over the next two years we will:

1. Implement comprehensive university-wide leadership for outreach and engagement that will:

- build capacity for outreach and engagement within departments and colleges;
- catalyze, support, catalogue, and publicize cross-cutting and college and department-level programs and their impacts;
- provide leadership for central initiatives;
- recognize and reward outstanding achievements in outreach and engagement;
- develop diversified revenue streams;
- and provide central support for and oversight of service learning.

The internal and external reviews of outreach and engagement have been completed. The President is reviewing these recommendations.

responsibility center: Office of the President.

2. Turn the vision of "live, learn, create, work communities" into a bold and viable business plan.

A team headed by Joe Alutto (Ohio State) and Rich Rosen (Battelle) prepared a preliminary proposal for the creation of the Columbus Center for the Arts and Sciences in the Lazarus building. A memorandum of understanding setting forth plans to work together on development of this project was signed in July 2004 by Ohio State, Battelle, and the Columbus Downtown Development Corporation.

responsibility center: Office of the President, Office of Research, Office of Outreach and Engagement.

3. Ask each college and regional campus to include in its pattern of administration a statement articulating how outreach and engagement activities are embedded in its teaching, research, and service and to designate a person responsible for coordinating those activities and for working with the Office of Outreach and Engagement.

responsibility center: colleges, Office of Academic Affairs, Office of Outreach and Engagement.

A.5. The Ohio State University Board of Trustees

2002–2003

Edward H. Jennings, Interim President
(July 1, 2002–September 30, 2002)

Karen A. Holbrook, President
(October 1, 2002–June 30, 2003)

BOARD OF TRUSTEES

	Term Beginning	Term Expiring
James F. Patterson, Chesterland	June 14, 1994	May 13, 2003
Zuheir Sofia, Columbus	May 14, 1995	May 13, 2004
Tami Longaberger, Nashport	May 14, 1996	May 13, 2005
Daniel M. Slane, Westerville	May 14, 1997	May 13, 2006
Robert M. Duncan, Columbus	May 19, 1998	May 13, 2007
Karen L. Hendricks, Cincinnati	May 14, 1999	May 13, 2008
Dimon R. McFerson, Powell	May 14, 2000	May 13, 2009
Jo Ann Davidson, Reynoldsburg	May 24, 2001	May 13, 2010
Douglas G. Borror, Dublin	May 24, 2002	May 13, 2011
Walden W. O'Dell, Canton	May 23, 2003	May 13, 2012
Joseph A. Shultz,* DeGraff	May 24, 2001	May 13, 2003
Paula A. Habib,* Columbus	May 24, 2002	May 13, 2004
Emily M. Quick,* Reynoldsburg	May 29, 2003	May 13, 2005

*Student Trustee – non voting

OFFICERS

James F. Patterson, Chairperson
Zuheir Sofia, Vice Chairperson
William J. Napier, Secretary, through September 6, 2002
Maureen T. Sharkey, Assistant Secretary, through December 5, 2002
David O. Frantz, Secretary, effective December 6, 2002
James L. Nichols, Treasurer

2003—2004

Karen A. Holbrook, President

BOARD OF TRUSTEES

	Term Beginning	Term Ending
Zuheir Sofia, Columbus	May 14, 1995	May 13, 2004
Tami Longaberger, Nashport	May 14, 1996	May 13, 2005
Daniel M. Slane, Westerville	May 14, 1997	May 13, 2006
Robert M. Duncan, Columbus	May 19, 1998	May 13, 2006
Karen L. Hendricks, Cincinnati	May 14, 1999	May 13, 2008
Dimon R. McFerson, Powell	May 14, 2000	May 13, 2009
Jo Ann Davidson, Reynoldsburg	May 24, 2001	May 13, 2010
Douglas G. Borror, Dublin	May 24, 2002	May 13, 2011
Walden W. O'Dell, Canton	May 23, 2003	May 13, 2012
Brian K. Hicks, Dublin	May 14, 2004	May 13, 2013
Paula A. Habib,* Columbus	May 24, 2002	May 13, 2004
Emily M. Quick,* Reynoldsburg	May 29, 2003	May 13, 2005
Chad A. Endsley,* Columbus	May 14, 2004	May 13, 2006

*Student Trustee – non voting

OFFICERS
Zuheir Sofia, Chairperson
Tami Longaberger, Vice Chairperson
David O. Frantz, Secretary
James L. Nichols, Treasurer

2004–2005

Karen A. Holbrook, President

BOARD OF TRUSTEES

	Term Beginning	Term Expiring
Tami Longaberger, Nashport	May 14, 1996	May 13, 2005
Daniel M. Slane, Westerville	May 14, 1997	May 13, 2006
Robert M. Duncan, Columbus	May 19, 1998	May 13, 2007
Karen L. Hendricks, Cincinnati	May 14, 1999	May 13, 2008
Dimon R. McFerson, Powell	May 14, 2000	May 13, 2009
Jo Ann Davidson, Reynoldsburg	May 24, 2001	May 13, 2010
Douglas G. Borror, Dublin	May 24, 2002	May 13, 2011
Walden W. O'Dell, Canton	May 23, 2003	May 13, 2012
Brian K. Hicks, Dublin	May 14, 2004	May 13, 2013
Emily M. Quick,* Reynoldsburg	May 29, 2003	May 13, 2005
Chad A. Endsley,* Columbus	May 14, 2004	May 13, 2006

*Student Trustee – non voting

OFFICERS
Tami Longaberger, Chairperson
Daniel M. Slane, Vice Chairperson
David O. Frantz, Secretary
James L. Nichols, Treasurer

2006–2007

Karen A. Holbrook, President

BOARD OF TRUSTEES

	Term Beginning	Term Expiring
Robert M. Duncan, Columbus	May 19, 1998	May 13, 2007
Karen L. Hendricks, Cincinnati	May 14, 1999	May 13, 2008
Dimon R. McFerson, Powell	May 14, 2000	May 13, 2009
G. Gilbert Cloyd, Cincinnati	December 30, 2005	May 13, 2009
Jo Ann Davidson, Reynoldsburg	May 24, 2001	May 13, 2010
John D. Ong, Hudson	December 30, 2005	May 13, 2010
Douglas G. Borror, Dublin	May 24, 2002	May 13, 2011
Leslie H. Wexner, New Albany	December 30, 2005	May 13, 2011
Walden W. O'Dell, Canton	May 23, 2003	May 13, 2012
Alex Shumate, Gahanna	May 26, 2006	May 13, 2012
Brian K. Hicks, Dublin	May 14, 2004	May 13, 2013
John C. "Jack" Fisher	July 21, 2006	May 13, 2013
Robert H. Schottenstein, Gahanna	July 1, 2005	May 13, 2014
Alan W. Brass, Toledo	July 21, 2006	May 13, 2014
Thekla R. Shackleford, Gahanna	May 26, 2006	May 13, 2015
Algenon L. Marbley, Columbus	May 31, 2007	May 13, 2016
Yoonhee Patricia Ha,* Columbus	July 1, 2005	May 13, 2007
Christopher A. Alvarez-Breckenridge,* Blacklick	June 9, 2006	May 13, 2008

*Student Trustee – non voting

OFFICERS

Robert M. Duncan, Chairperson
Karen L. Hendricks, Vice Chairperson
David O. Frantz, Secretary
Thomas W. Johnson, Interim Treasurer, appointed 2/2/07

A.6. Foundation Board Members, 2002–2007

Amstutz, Dan (11/98 3 yrs)
Arthur, William (11/06 3 yrs)
Aveni, Vince (11/97 3 yrs)
   died 9/22/06
Berry Jr., John (11/99 3 yrs)
Chen, Chih-Ming (11/05 3 yrs)
Coleman, Kenneth (11/06 3 yrs)
Cooperman, Ed (11/96 3 yrs)
Crane, Jameson (1991, 3 yrs)
Crane, Loann (11/94 3 yrs)
Creighton Jr., Jack (11/01 3 yrs)
Davis, Samuel B. (11/01 3 yrs)
Denman, Richard (1985, 3 yrs)
Ernst, Ruann (11/01 3 yrs)
Fergus, Barbara (11/06 3 yrs)
Gasper, Joseph (11/99 3 yrs.)
Gerlach, Jay (11/97 3 yrs)
Glimcher, Herb (2001, 3 year)
Groves, Ray (11/94 3 yrs)
Hagenlocker, Ed (11/99 3 yrs)
Hull, Virginia (1986, 3 year)
Hummel, Robert (11/02 3 yrs)
Ingram, Bill (11/99 3 yrs)
Isaac, Bill (11/99 3 yrs.)
Jacobs, Alexis A. (11/99 3 yrs)
Kent, Ralph
Kessler, Jack (5/85; 5/95 3 yrs ea.)
Klatskin, Charles (11/00 3 yrs)
Klingbeil, Jim (11/97 3 yrs)
Kravinsky, Zell (11/04 3 yrs)
Krimendahl, Fred (11/99 3 yrs)

Krueger, Cheryl (11/06 3 yrs)
Levitt, Maddie (11/04 3 yrs)
   died 11/7/07
Lowrie, Bill (11/96 3 yrs)
Lucks, Jack (11/99 3 yrs)
Martini, Robert (11/96 3 yrs)
Mason Jr., Ray (11/98 3 yrs)
McCoy, John G. (1985, 3 yrs)
Moritz, Michael E. (1990, 3 yrs)
Moritz, Lou Ann (11/02 3 yrs)
Murrer, Martin (11/05 3 yrs)
Pfahl, Floradelle (11/98 3 yrs)
Price, Corbett (11/01 3 yrs)
Reusche, Robert (11/01 3 yrs)
Rismiller, David (11/02 3 yrs)
Robinson, Patricia (11/97 3 yrs)
Rockow, Ralph (11/01 3 yrs)
Sandefur, John (11/00 3 yrs)
Schiff Jr., John J. (11/01 3 yrs)
Schoenbaum, Betty (5/97 3 yrs)
Shackelford, Teckie (11/94 3 yrs)
Sharrock, David (1985, 3 yrs)
Shepherd, John (11/97 3 yrs)
Shumate, Alex (11/98 3 yrs)
Tata, Ratan (11/05 3 yrs)
Trueman, Barbara (11/94 3 yrs)
Wells, William (11/04 3 yrs)
Wolfe, John F. (11/97 3 yrs)
Wolstein, Bertram (2003, 3 yrs)
Wolstein, Iris (11/04 3 yrs)
Wobst, Frank (2/91 3 yrs)
Woods, Jackie (1996, 3 yrs)

A.7. Faculty Leadership

CHAIRS OF THE SENATE STEERING COMMITTEE

Year	Chair
2002–3	Stanley C. Ahalt
2003–4	Stephen S. Pinsky
2004–5	David G. Horn
2005–6	Anthony Mughan
2006–7	Harald Vaessin

CHAIRS OF FACULTY COUNCIL

Year	Chair
2002–3	Gene E. Mumy
2003–4	Grady W. Chism
2004–5	Jack A. Rall
2005–6	Philip T.K. Daniel
2006–7	Allan Silverman

SECRETARIES OF THE UNIVERSITY SENATE

Year	Chair
2000–2005	Susan W. Fisher
2005–11	Christian K. Zacher

A.8. Members of the President's Cabinet

2002 MEMBERS

Karen A. Holbrook
President

William H. Hall
Vice President for Student Affairs

Jerry A. May
Vice President for University Development

C. Bradley Moore
Vice President for Research

Bobby D. Moser
Vice President for Agricultural Administration and University Outreach
Executive Dean, College of Food, Agricultural, and Environmental Sciences

William J. Napier
Acting Vice President for Government Relations

Edward J. Ray
Executive Vice President and Provost

Fred Sanfilippo
Senior Vice President for Health Sciences
Dean, College of Medicine and Public Health

William J. Shkurti
Senior Vice President for Business and Finance

Barbara R. Snyder
Interim Vice President for University Relations

Mac A. Stewart
Vice Provost for Minority Affairs

Virginia M. Trethewey
Executive Assistant to the President and General Counsel

David O. Frantz *(ex officio)*
Secretary of the Board of Trustees

2007 MEMBERS

Karen A. Holbrook
President

Joseph A. Alutto
Executive Dean, Professional Colleges
Dean, Fisher College of Business

Christopher M. Culley
Vice President for Legal Affairs and General Counsel

Evelyn B. Freeman
Executive Dean, Regional Campuses
Dean and Director, Ohio State Mansfield

Peter E. Geier
Vice President for Health Services
Chief Executive Officer, OSU Health System
Chief Operating Officer, OSU Medical Center

Richard A. Hollingsworth
Vice President for Student Affairs

Larry M. Lewellen
Associate Vice President for Human Resources

Robert T. McGrath
Senior Vice President for Research

Susan E. Metros
Interim Chief Information Officer

Bobby D. Moser
Vice President for Agricultural Administration and University Outreach
Executive Dean, College of Food, Agricultural, and Environmental Sciences

Jacqueline J. Royster
Senior Vice Provost
Executive Dean, Colleges of the Arts and Sciences

Fred Sanfilippo
Senior Vice President and Executive Dean for Health Sciences
Chief Executive Officer, OSU Medical Center

James C. Schroeder
Vice President for University Development

William J. Shkurti
Senior Vice President for Business and Finance

Gene D. Smith
Director of Athletics

Barbara R. Snyder
Executive Vice President and Provost

Curt Steiner
Senior Vice President for University Relations

Mac A. Stewart
Vice Provost for Minority Affairs
Special Assistant to the President for Diversity

Christian K. Zacher
Secretary of the University Senate

Pearl M. Bigfeather *(ex officio)*
Chief of Staff and Special Assistant to the President

David O. Frantz *(ex officio)*
Secretary of the Board of Trustees

A.9. Honorary Degree Recipients, 2002–2007

Date Conferred	Name	Degree Conferred
March 22, 2002	Wilford Robert Gardner	D. Science
	Theodore M. Hesburgh	D. Humane Letters
	Ray D. Owen	D. Science
June 12, 2002	F. Sherwood Rowland (special ceremony, Research Lecture Series)	D. Science
June 14, 2002	George W. Bush	D. Public Admin.
	Walter E. Massey	D. Science
	George M. Steinbrenner II	D. Bus. Admin.
	Marta Tienda	D. Social Science
August 30, 2002	Harold A. McMaster	D. Science
	André Wambersie	D. Science
November 4, 2002	Yuan T. Lee (special ceremony, Research Lecture Series)	D. Science
December 13, 2002	Charles Augustus Ballard	D. Public Service
	Howard E. LeFevre	D. Humane Letters
	Louis W. Sullivan	D. Public Health
March 13, 2003	Martha Craven Nussbaum (special ceremony, Research Lecture Series)	D. Humane Letters
March 21, 2003	Eva Klein	D. Science
	Elizabeth M. Ross	D. Humane Letters
	Arthur M. Schlesinger, Jr.	D. Humane Letters
May 13, 2003	David McCullough (special ceremony, Research Lecture Series)	D. Humane Letters

Date Conferred	Name	Degree Conferred
June 13, 2003	Robert D. Havener	D. Public Service
	Adrienne L. Kennedy	D. Literature
	William E. Kirwan	D. Education
	R.E. "Ted" Turner	D. Humane Letters
	William F. Ganong	D. Science
	Dennis J. Greenland	D. Science
August 29, 2003	Thomas R. Cech (special ceremony, Research Lecture Series)	D. Science
October 1, 2003	Gerardus 't Hooft	D. Science
	Nathaniel R. Jones	D. Law
	Mark B. Rucker	D. Music
December 14, 2003	Avery Cardinal Dulles, S.J.	D. Humane Letters
	Durbin Duran Feeling	D. Humane Letters
March 21, 2004	David W. Harvey	D. Science
June 13, 2004	Ernest M. Henley	D. Science
August 29, 2004	Howard M. Johnson	D. Science
December 12, 2004	Edward J. Larson	D. Humane Letters
	Leon M. Lederman	D. Science Education
	M.S. Swaminathan	D. Agricultural Science
March 20, 2005	Gerald E. Brown	D. Science
	Eugenie C. Scott	D. Science
June 12, 2005	Glen H. Elder, Jr.	D. Social Science
	William H. Hall	D. Public Service
	Carl E. Wieman	D. Science
August 28, 2005	Frank M. Bass	D. Bus. Admin.
	Roger O. McClellan	D. Science
	Grayce McVeigh Sills	D. Public Service

Date Conferred	Name	Degree Conferred
December 11, 2005	Judah Folkman	D. Science
	Jerome I. Friedman	D. Science
March 19, 2006	Neta A. Bahcall	D. Science
	Shirley A. Jackson	D. Science
	Gurdev S. Khush	D. Science
June 11, 2006	Alan J. Heeger	D. Science
	Alan G. MacDiarmid	D. Science
August 27, 2006	None	
December 10, 2006	T.R. Lakshmanan	D. Science
	Douglas D. Osheroff	D. Science
	Roy R. Romer	D. Public Service
	Pedro A. Sanchez	D. Science
March 18, 2007	Archibald O. Haller, Jr.	D. Social Science
	Shirley M. Malcom	D. Science
June 10, 2007	Gerald D. Buckberg	D. Science
	Jean-Pierre G. Changeux	D. Science
	William J. Clinton	D. Public Service
	Gilberto Gil Moreira	D. Music
	Karen A. Holbrook	D. Education
August 26, 2007	David J. Gross	D. Science
	Orlando L. Taylor	D. Higher Education
August 28, 2007	Vladan Radovanovic (special ceremony in Serbia)	D. Music
December 9, 2007	Wolfgang Ketterle	D. Science
	John M. Opitz	D. Science

A.10. Wexner Prize Winners, 2002–2007

2002 – William Forsythe
2004 – Issey Miyake
2005 – Bill T. Jones

A.11. Commencement Speakers, 2002–2007

2002

March   **David L. Brennan,** Chair, Board of Trustees, The Ohio State University

June   **George W. Bush,** 43rd President of the United States

August   **Roger D. Blackwell,** Professor of Marketing, The Ohio State University

December   **Louis W. Sullivan,** President Emeritus, Morehouse School of Medicine, and Former U.S. Secretary of Health and Human Services

2003

March   **Geoffrey Parker,** Andreas Dorpalen Professor of History and Associate of the Mershon Center, The Ohio State University

June   **Christopher Reeve,** Chairman, The Christopher Reeve Paralysis Foundation

August   **Carl F. Kohrt,** President and CEO, Battelle Memorial Institute

December   **M. Marnette Perry,** Senior Vice President, The Kroger Company

2004

March   **Lonnie G. Thompson,** Distinguished University Professor, Department of Geological Sciences, The Ohio State University

June   **Erin F. Moriarty,** CBS News Correspondent

August   **Lee S. Shulman,** President, Carnegie Foundation for the Advancement of Teaching

December   **Deborah Jones Merritt,** Director, The John Glenn Institute for Public Service and Public Policy, The Ohio State University

2005

March   **Eugenie C. Scott,** Executive Director, National Center for Science Education

June	**William H. Hall,** Vice President for Student Affairs, The Ohio State University
August	**Jodie T. Allen,** Senior Editor, The Pew Research Center
December	**Deborah A. Ballam,** Associate Provost for Women's Policy Initiatives, Director, The Women's Place, Professor, Fisher College of Business, The Ohio State University

2006

March	**Shirley Ann Jackson,** President, Rensselaer Polytechnic Institute
June	**John McCain,** United States Senator
August	**Robert J. Massie,** President, Chemical Abstracts Service
December	**Roy R. Romer,** Former Governor of Colorado

2007

March	**Joseph H. Lynch,** Distinguished University Professor and Joe R. Engle Designated Professor of the History of Christianity, The Ohio State University
June	**William J. Clinton,** 42nd President of the United States
August	**Michael F. Curtin,** Vice Chair and Associate Publisher, *The Columbus Dispatch*
December	**Brian D. Joseph,** Distinguished University Professor of Linguistics and Kenneth E. Naylor Professor of South Slavic Linguistics, The Ohio State University

A.12. Total Private Support During the Holbrook Administration

Fiscal Year	Amount Contributed
2002	$179,492,686
2003	$195,759,414
2004	$206,078,029
2005	$206,160,133
2006	$211,316,845
2007	$228,195,143

A.13. Campus Construction Begun and Completed Under Holbrook

Project Name	Approx. Budget (in millions)	Notes
Lane Avenue Parking Garage	$30.90	Design began 9/2006
Student Academic Services Building	$32.00	Design began 9/2006
OARDC Animal & Plant Biology Level 3 Isolate Facility	$23.60	Design began 8/2007
MCFP Expansion Projects	$1,000.00	Approved by Board 11/2005
Cunz Hall Renovation	$24.30	Design approved by Board 4/2007
Women's Softball Stadium	$5.60	Bidding approved by Board 2/2007
650 Ackerman Road Renovation	$20.00	Renovation work started 2/2003
McCracken Power Plant Chiller Expansion	$13.40	Construction started 6/2004
North Doan Hall Non-Clinical Addition and Digestive Health Center (MCFP)	$33.50	Construction started 11/2005
Ohio Union Replacement	$118.80	Construction started 1/2007
Ohio Union Garage Renovation and Expansion	$21.00	Construction started 5/2007
Ross Heart Hospital Two Floor Addition (MCFP)	$27.30	Construction started 5/2007
Thompson Library Renovation	$110.00	Under construction 11/2007

Project Name	Approx. Budget (in millions)	Notes
Library Book Depository Phase II	$2.30	Completed 12/2002
Wetland Research and Education Building	$2.00	Completed 2/2003
Aronoff Laboratory (formerly Life Sciences Research Building)	$24.60	Completed 5/2003
Byrd Polar Research Center Rock Repository	$0.70	Completed 7/2003
Sisson Hall Replacement	$29.10	Completed 7/2003
Graduate and Professional Student Housing	$33.30	Completed 9/2003
Wiseman Hall Comprehensive Cancer Center Expansion	$9.10	Completed 3/2004
Hospitals Parking Garage	$16.60	Completed 7/2004
Knowlton School of Architecture	$33.00	Completed 7/2004
Hagerty Hall Rehabilitation	$25.40	Completed 10/2004
Page Hall Renovation	$16.30	Completed 10/2004
Neil Avenue Garage	$14.90	Completed 11/2004
Ross Heart Hospital	$63.40	Completed 11/2004
Student Family Community Center at Buckeye Village	$5.70	Completed 12/2004
Physical Sciences Research Building	$59.00	Completed 3/2005
Psychology Building	$34.00	Completed 1/2006

Project Name	Approx. Budget (in millions)	Notes
West Campus Biocontainment Laboratory	$2.90	Completed 3/2006
Mechanical Engineering Building Replacement (Robinson Lab Replacement)	$67.20	Completed 8/2006
Fry Hall Addition	$9.30	Completed 10/2006
Biomedical Research Tower	$120.70	Completed 12/2006
Laboratory Animal Facilities	$15.50	Completed 12/2006
Larkins Hall Replacement	$155.40	Completed 12/2006
Jennings Hall Renovation (Botany and Zoology Renovation)	$33.60	Construction completed 7/2007
Early Childhood Development Center at Weinland Park	$9.60	Completed 8/2007
Woody Hayes Athletic Center Renovation	$19.00	Completed 8/2007
Ohio 4-H Center	$13.40	Completed 11/2007

A.14. Selections from Holbrook's Weekly Calendar, 2002 and 2007

November 18 – November 24

November 2002

S	M	T	W	T	F	S
					1	2
3	4	5	6	7	8	9
10	11	12	13	14	15	16
17	18	19	20	21	22	23
24	25	26	27	28	29	30

December 2002

S	M	T	W	T	F	S
1	2	3	4	5	6	7
8	9	10	11	12	13	14
15	16	17	18	19	20	21
22	23	24	25	26	27	28
29	30	31				

Monday, November 18

The Mark Hotel (Madison Ave & E. 77th St. , 212-744-4300, fax: 212-744-4300)

7:30am 7:55am 7:30am Midge Stulberg will meet you in the hotel lobby
8:00am 8:50am 8am Breakfast meeting /w Ray Groves at his office (1166 Avenue of the
9:00am 9:45am 9am Stephen Swid (152 W. 57th Street, 57th Floor, between 6th and 7th
10:00am 10:45am Fred Krimendahl (630 Fifth Avenue, Suite 3170 (at 51st Street) 212-977-3712)
11:00am 11:45am 11am Erin Moriarty and Andrew Heyward - CANCELLED (CBS Studios, 524 W.
12:00pm 1:15pm 12N Lunch /w Alan Patricof, /w Jerry May, Midge Stulberg (Pazo Restaurant,
2:00pm 2:45pm 2pm Bob Dilenschneider (200 Park Avenue, 212-922-0900)
3:00pm 4:00pm OPEN: You will return to The Mark Hotel
4:00pm 5:00pm 4:00pm Tea /w Corbett Price (The Holbrook's suite, The Mark Hotel)
5:00pm 5:50pm OPEN - Hotel Checkout
6:00pm 6:30pm 6:00pm Wine with Lynn and Charlie Klatskin (Mark's Bar at the Mark Hotel)
More Items...

Tuesday, November 19

9:00am 11:00am 9:00am INTRO: P&P Diversity Lecture Series–Faith & Diversity in American Religion" Alan Wolfe (Ohio Union, Conference Theater, 2nd Floor, 1739 North
11:30am 12:30pm 11:30am REMARKS: President's International Leadership Luncheon (Faculty Club, West Dining Room)
1:00pm 1:15pm Elizabeth Consisk
1:15pm 1:30pm 1:15pm Jan Greenwood to call you
1:45pm 2:30pm 1:45pm Jerry May, Amb. John Ong, chair emeritus of B.F. Goodrich & current US Amb. to Norway (205 Bricker Hall)
2:30pm 3:00pm 2:30pm Bill Shkurti Pre-Board
3:00pm 3:15pm 3pm Dave Bhaerman re. pp
3:15pm 5:15pm OTP Office
5:30pm 6:30pm 5:30pm KH/JH: Patrick Wadsworth, Ann, Landscaping and Design Students re. Holiday decorations (residence)

Wednesday, November 20

8:00am 11:00am Cabinet (200 Bricker Hall)
11:30am 11:00am Sikurti, Moser, Ray, Trethewey (205 Bricker Hall)
11:30am 12:45pm 11:30am Lunch with President's Council on Women's Issues (Faculty Club, West Dining Room)
1:00pm 1:30pm 1:00pm Donna Evans, dean of education
2:00pm 2:30pm Dave Bhaerman re. PowerPoint
2:45pm 3:45pm 2:45pm REMARKS: Reception for international students majoring in the Humanities (136 University Hall (in the Crane eCafe), 230 N Oval Mall)
4:45pm 5:00pm Tom to take you to the Legislative Reception
5:00pm 6:00pm REMARKS: Legislative reception (Capital Club)
6:00pm 6:30pm Mr. Sofia to drive you home
7:00pm 8:30pm KAH/JAH Dinner /w Jim and Nancy Patterson Buca Dibeppo (343 North Front Street, 621-3287)

Thursday, November 21

For President Holbrook's information, the Board's Fiscal Affairs Committee will have their annual Audit

8:15am 8:30am Tom to pick you up at the residence
8:30am 10:00am 8:30am Black Ministers Breakfast w/ Bill Hall & Mac Stewart (Trinity Baptist.
10:30am 11:10am Hospital Board Meeting (5th Floor Prior Health Sciences Library - Tom to drive)
11:15am 11:30am Tom to pick up and take you to the Faculty Club
11:30am 1:00pm HOLD: Lunch with Paul Asteford, president, Columbus Convention Center OR
11:30am 12:45pm 11:30am AAUP (Faculty Club, Room A)
12:45pm 1:00pm Tom to pick you up and take you to WOSU
1:00pm 2:00pm 1pm Open Line with Fred Andrie (WOSU Stations)
2:00pm 2:30pm 2pm Viewpoint Taping (WOSU Stations)
2:00pm 2:15pm Viewpoint Taping (WOSU Stations)
2:30pm 3:00pm 2:30pm Michigan Press Conference Taping (WOSU)
More Items...

Friday, November 22

FYI: 7:30pm Men's BB vs. Harlem Globetrotters

7:10am 7:25am Call in to the Bob Connors Show 610-WTVN radio re. fan behavior (488-2483)
8:00am 9:00am 8am Fred Sanfilippo (205 Bricker)
9:00am 10:00am Randall "Rip" Ripley (205 Bricker)
9:00am 9:30am 9am Randall "Rip" Ripley (205 Bricker)
9:30am 10:30am 9:30am Ginny, Michelle, Mary (205 Bricker)
10:30am 1:30pm 10:30am Rotary Speech Preparation
1:30pm 2:15pm 1:30pm John Bruno re: EOCA
1:30pm 2:15pm John Bruno re: EOCA
2:15pm 2:45pm 2:15pm Frank Hale (205 Bricker)
3:00pm 3:30pm 3pm Lee Tashjian (205 Bricker)
4:00pm 4:20pm Maureen, Ginny, David Frantz re. Pre-Board
More Items...

Saturday, November 23

8:45am 9:00am 8:45am Tom to pick up at the residence
9:30am 11:30am 9:30am President's Brunch (Drake Union - Tom driving)
11:30am 11:50am 11:30am WBNS Television (Lee will take you from brunch to the field for
12:15pm 12N Ohio State v. Michigan
2:15pm 2:45pm Halftime: Skip Mosic interview
More Items...

Sunday, November 24

9:00am 10:00am Meeting with Administration re. Off Campus Riots
1:30pm 1:45pm Press Conference: Student Affairs re. Off Campus Riots (33 West 11th Avenue)
2:30pm 2:45pm FYI: Mike Adams Departs CMH - Delta 1679

June 04 – June 10

	June 2007							July 2007				
S	M	T	W	T	F	S	S	M	T	W	T	F	S
					1	2	1	2	3	4	5	6	7
3	4	5	6	7	8	9	8	9	10	11	12	13	14
10	11	12	13	14	15	16	15	16	17	18	19	20	21
17	18	19	20	21	22	23	22	23	24	25	26	27	28
24	25	26	27	28	29	30	29	30	31				

Monday, June 04

7:30am	Breakfast w/Carl Kohrt (Panera, South Campus Gateway, 1619 N. High St.)
9:30am	10:00am Mohan Wall--10 minutes (205 Bricker)
10:00am	10:30am David F, Chris C, Curt S (205 Bricker)
10:30am	11:30am Fred S. (205 Bricker)
12:00pm	1:30pm Lunch w/Ginny T. (Lindey's), she will pick you up
2:00pm	2:30pm Chris Z. stopping by, with Univ Senate gift (205 Bricker)
2:00pm	3:00pm Michael Crow conference call (they will call us)
3:30pm	4:30pm Ohio Staters Inc. reception (Faculty Club, Main Dining Room)
5:00pm	5:30pm Columbus City Council recognition event (Council chambers, 90 W Broad)
5:30pm	6:00pm Mike Bowersock interview for Channel 4, after City Council
7:00pm	8:30pm Dinner w/Fred & Janet Sanfilippo, their home (422 N. Parkview Ave.)

Tuesday, June 05

7:30am	8:30am breakfast w/Jack Kessler (Columbus Club, 181 E. Broad St)
8:30am	10:00am Kathy Underwood at Residence
10:30am	11:00am Peter Magrath calling you
11:00am	11:30am Randy S.--5 min. (205 Bricker)
11:30am	12:00pm Barbara S. (205 Bricker)
12:00pm	1:00pm Susan Metros (Faculty Club), she'll stop by here
2:00pm	3:00pm Mike Caligiuri (205 Bricker)
4:00pm	5:00pm Jim S, Chris C, Bob McG, Tom Johnson, Joe Irvine, Tim Michel (205 Bricker)

Wednesday, June 06

7:30am	9:30am Wise Women breakfast, Deloitte & Touche (Blackwell)
10:00am	11:00am Metro High School reception, Tyler Schuch attending--Tom to drive (1929 Kenny Rd)
12:00pm	1:30pm Lunch with Vinita Mehra & Martijn Steger (Capital Club)--Tom to drive
2:00pm	3:00pm Carrie Ghose, Business First interview w/Shelly H. (205 Bricker)
4:00pm	6:00pm Farewell reception for Barbara Snyder (Blackwell, Ballrooms A-C)
6:00pm	8:30pm dinner w/Barbara and Michael

Thursday, June 07

Overnight: Bethesda Marriott Hotel, 5151 Pooks Hill Rd, ph:301-897-9400

Time	Event
8:00am	9:00am 7:30am Breakfast w/David Cheseborough (Capital Club)
9:30am	10:30am 9:30am Bob Massie (205 Bricker)--cone out front
10:30am	11:00am 10:30am visit by Army ROTC, gift presentation (205 Bricker)
11:30am	12:30pm 11:30am Scitech board meeting (1275 Kinnear Rd)
12:30pm	2:00pm 12:30pm Lunch w/Gil Cloyd, Fred (205 Bricker)
2:00pm	3:00pm 2:15pm Groundbreaking for Neighborhood Policing Center (248 E. 11th Ave, between Summit and N. Fourth Sts)--Tom to drive
3:30pm	4:00pm 3:30pm interview by Carol Luper, w/Shelly H. (205 Bricker)
4:00pm	7:00pm HOLD
7:00pm	7:30pm 7:05pm Depart on US Airways #3070
8:30pm	9:30pm 8:39pm Arrive Washington National. Take taxi to hotel, Bethesda Marriott, 5151 Pooks Hill Rd.

Friday, June 08

FYI--Embry-Riddle board retreat (The Greenbrier, White Sulphur Springs, WV)

NIH ACD meeting (Bethesda, MD)

Time	Event
8:30am	5:30pm NIH Advisory Committee to the Director meeting 8:30a-5:30p (NIH offices, Bethesda MD)
8:30pm	9:00pm 8:57pm Depart Washington Nat'l on US Airways #3417
10:00pm	10:30pm 10:17pm Arrive Columbus.

Saturday, June 09

FYI--Embry-Riddle board retreat (The Greenbrier, White Sulphur Springs, WV)

FYI--Fisher College of Business MBA graduation ceremony (Mershon Auditorium)

Time	Event
8:00am	3:30pm HOLD
3:30pm	4:00pm 3:30 pm robing for convocation
4:00pm	5:00pm 4:00pm Optometry Convocation (Drake Union)
6:00pm	8:30pm 6:00pm pre-commencement dinner (Longaberger)

Sunday, June 10

Embassy Suites Convention Center, 999 9th St NW, ph:202-719-1421

FYI--ACGME executive committee and CILE meetings

Time	Event
8:30am	9:00am 8:30am Anna will pick group up at Residence
9:00am	10:00am 9:00am Army ROTC spring commissioning ceremony (Knowlton Hall
11:00am	11:30am 11:00am stop by, SASSO brunch, Recruiting Room, Ohio Stadium)

More Items....

About the Author

Christian Zacher has held a number of administrative positions at Ohio State—director of the Center for Medieval and Renaissance Studies, associate dean of Humanities, chair of Comparative Studies, and secretary of the University Senate. Educated at Holy Cross College and the University of California, Riverside, he has been a faculty member in English at OSU since 1968. He is author or co-editor of books and articles on medieval literature and the American Midwest. He is now an emeritus professor, and lives in Columbus with his wife, Kay Bea Jones, an associate professor of Architecture, and their son Sam.

Index

www.ingramcontent.com/pod-product-compliance
Lightning Source LLC
LaVergne TN
LVHW091200080426
835509LV00006B/761